THE COMPLETE KETO DIET COOKBOOK FOR BEGINNERS 2019

Mandy Cook

CONTENTS

INTRODUCTION 5

What is the Keto Diet?................... 7

Consider Macronutrient
Balance................................12

6 Critical Ketogenic Diet Tips 15

3 Proven Benefits of a
Ketogenic Diet............................19

A Few Hacks You Might
Benefit From 20

3- Weak Meal Plan........................21

All about Our Recipe Collection.. 27

VEGETABLES & SIDE DISHES ..28

1. Cauliflower, Ham and
Cheese Bake 29

2. Creamy Broccoli and
Bacon Soup 30

3. Spinach with Paprika and
Cheese 31

4. Cheesy Zucchini Casserole...... 32

5. Stuffed Peppers with
Cauliflower and Cheese............... 33

6. Chinese-Style Cauliflower
Rice 34

7. Spicy Baked Eggplant with
Herbs and Cheese 35

8. The Best Zucchini
Fritters Ever 36

9. Stuffed Spaghetti
Squash Bowls................................37

POULTRY 38

10. Tangy Classic Chicken
Drumettes..................................... 39

11. Easy Turkey Curry.................. 40

12. Ranch Chicken Breasts
with Cheese 41

13. Cheesy Chicken
Drumsticks 42

14. Special Chicken Salad 43

15. Turkey Crust Pizza
with Bacon 44

16. Old-Fashioned
Chicken Soup 45

17. Crispy Chicken Filets in
Tomato Sauce 46

18. Lemon Garlic Grilled
Chicken Wings 47

PORK **48**

19. Mexican-Style Pork Tacos 49

20. Pork Cutlets in Chili Tangy Sauce 50

21. Holiday Pork Belly with Vegetables 51

22. Cheeseburger Skillet with Bacon and Mushrooms 52

23. Country-Style Pork Stew 53

24. Cheesy and Buttery Pork Chops 54

25. Filipino Nilaga Soup 55

26. Pork Tenderloin with Southern Cabbage 56

27. Indian-Style Fried Pork 57

BEEF 58

28. Italian-Style Spicy Meatballs 59

29. Rich Double-Cheese Meatloaf 60

30. Meat and Goat Cheese Stuffed Mushrooms 61

31. Shredded Beef with Herbs 62

32. Chinese Ground Beef Skillet 63

33. Easy Steak Salad 64

34. Saucy Skirt Steak with Broccoli 65

35. Classic Beef Stroganoff 66

FISH & SEAFOOD **67**

36. Catfish and Cauliflower Casserole 68

37. Swedish Herring Salad 69

38. Hearty Fisherman's Stew 70

39. Fish and Vegetable Medley 71

40. Salmon Curry with a Twist 72

41. Tuna, Avocado and Ham Wraps 73

42. Alaskan Cod with Mustard Cream Sauce 74

43. Smoked Haddock Fish Burgers 75

EGGS & DAIRY **76**

44. Paprika Omelet with Goat Cheese 77

45. Dilly Boiled Eggs with Avocado 78

46. Greek-Style Frittata with Herbs 79

47. Mangalorean Egg Curry 80

48. Egg, Bacon and Kale Muffins 81

49. Cheesy Brussels Sprouts 82

50. Cauliflower, Cheese and Egg Fat Bombs 83

51. Double Cheese and Sausage Balls 84

VEGETARIAN 85

52. Mexican Inspired Stuffed Peppers 86

53. Frittata with Asparagus and Halloumi 87

54. Baked Eggs and Cheese in Avocado.. 88

55. Two-Cheese Zucchini Gratin 89

56. Italian Zuppa di Pomodoro.... 90

57. Two-Cheese and Kale Bake ...91

58. Grandma's Zucchini and Spinach Chowder 92

59. Crêpes with Peanut Butter and Coconut 93

SNACKS & APPETIZERS...........94

60. Lettuce Wraps with Ham and Cheese 95

61. Ranch and Blue Cheese Dip..................................... 96

62. Ranch Chicken Wings 97

63. Colby Cheese-Stuffed Meatballs 98

64. Cheese and Artichoke Dip 99

65. Italian Cheese Crisps 100

66. Deviled Eggs with Mustard and Chives 101

67. Mini Stuffed Peppers.............102

DESSERTS 103

68. Almond Butter and Chocolate Cookies 104

69. Basic Orange Cheesecake.....105

70. Peanut Butter and Chocolate Treat...........................106

71. Coconut Cranberry Bars 107

72. Peanut and Butter Cubes......108

73. Easiest Brownies Ever 109

74. No Bake Party Cake 110

75. Vanilla Mug Cake 111

INTRODUCTION

I have struggled with my weight almost my whole life, since my teenage years. I've been on a diet since I was 14. I was always hungry; I didn't have a good night's sleep and energy for my daily tasks and activities. Shortly after that, I got stuck in a cycle of "yo-yo dieting" or weight gain followed by weight loss. I spent many years feeling out of control with my eating. I felt that I was disconnected from my own body and I didn't listen to it but I cannot help myself. As a teenager of 16, I struggled with depression. I felt devastated; my friends could not understand how this straight-A student and beautiful girl could have any mental problems. In addition, my parents did not understand what I was going through; they thought I went through a phase like other teens with fluctuating emotions. Later, when I was in college, my struggles continued. I was dieting, sometimes successfully sometimes not. It is like a hamster on its wheel!

When I graduated college, I had everything I thought I wanted. Nevertheless, I wasn't happy. I had an almost phobic fear of food, especially greasy food, nuts, and fatty cheese. This belief about fats is based on a common fact that we have heard so many times so we just assume it is true. It is like many other ideas that fall into the category of "myths" that are totally wrong! Ironically, natural food, including natural fats, is good for the human body. In theory, if you want to lose weight, you should burn more calories than you eat; you should also pay attention to regular physical activities, take the stairs instead of elevators, walk an extra 30 minutes a day, blah, blah, blah... Easier said than done. In practice, we should analyze many factors to understand that there are often more than one cause of weight gain. Psychological factors, genetic predisposition, food addiction, high insulin levels, hormone imbalance, and neurologic problems all may play a part.

When I look back on my life, I see low self-esteem and misery. I also thought that cooking at home is time-consuming so I regularly ordered food delivery. I decided to stop torturing myself and break the starve-binge cycle. I decided to be happy! "Everything in your life is a reflection of a choice you have made. If you want a different result, make a different choice," said Anonymous. So, I asked myself, "What make you feel persistently hungry, despite eating enough food and three meals a day? What are you doing to your body!? What should you do if you want to feel and look your best?" These questions were complicated for me, but deep in my heart, I knew that the answers were simple. Luckily, I found the answers and heal my relationship with food.

Three years ago, I had discovered a low-carb dietary regimen. It is a low carbohydrate, moderate protein, and high fat based diet. Basically, I can eat meat, poultry, eggs and dairy on a keto diet and avoid rice, grains and legumes. I was skeptical at first, it sounds too good to be true! Fortunately, I was proven wrong, this nutrition plan is better than I've ever expected. My goal with this recipe collection is to show you an easy but effective way to kickstart a ketogenic diet. Also, I wanted to use my experience and knowledge to encourage you on your keto adventure with all ins and outs. After years of struggle, I feel optimistic and inspired to pay it forward and help others to find their path to a happy life. If you feel overwhelmed or intimidated, whatever you are going through, I am here to tell you that everything is possible; so, never give up. If I can do it, you can too!

WHAT IS THE KETO DIET?

According to Wikipedia, "A ketogenic diet is a diet that derives most of its calories from fat and only a small number of calories from carbohydrates. The diet forces the body to burn fats rather than carbohydrates for energy. Normally, the carbohydrates you eat are turned into glucose in the body, which is used for energy around the body and in the brain. But, if you don't eat enough carbohydrates, your body has a back-up system of burning fat instead. The liver can use stored fat and the fat you eat for energy. Stored fat is broken into two parts, fatty acids, and ketone bodies. Ketone bodies power the brain instead of glucose. This state of having a lot of ketone bodies in your blood is called Ketosis."

When I discovered a keto lifestyle, something about it really inspired me to do detailed research. I read a lot of articles and studies, seeing real people getting real and great results; then, I put theory into practice and Voilà! I did it! And I did it well! A month after starting this amazing lifestyle, my life completely changed.

I started following a ketogenic diet with a daily calorie breakdown of 5% carbs, 20% protein, and 75% fats. I also tried to stay within my calorie needs. It is not difficult since a common symptom of this diet is the feeling of fullness. The appetite suppression may be linked to a higher intake of fat and protein. My ultimate goal was to boost the body's metabolism to speed up my weight loss. Besides being in ketosis, I tried to make some changes to help rev up my metabolism. Some of these changes include eating a good breakfast, doing simple exercises to build muscles, eating protein with every meal, drinking green tea, and adding hot peppers to my meals. "Do not skip meals" is one of the best tips I've ever heard since skipping meals, especially breakfast, can cause the metabolism to slow down.

Once I reached my ideal weight, I tried to rotate very low carbohydrate days with higher carbohydrate days so I can say that simple plan works for me. Alternatively, you can keep on with your keto lifestyle, but you can eat a little more food for weight maintenance. You can add a little more protein but keep carbs low. You can add more carbs only before and after workouts. It is advisable to go slowly, and raise your daily carb limit by 10 to 20 grams for a week or two, and stick with Paleo foods. In this phase, you can eat carbs that are nutrient-dense and fiber-rich such as carrots, peppers, potatoes, turnips, pears, bananas, oranges, and strawberries. Another great way to maintain your goal weight is to combine intermittent fasting with muscle-gaining keto. The key is just to find that perfect amount of food for your body, age, and activity level. Most people, including me, do not have to be in ketosis to stay at a healthy weight, as long as they stick with a low-carb diet such as Paleo, LCHF or low-carb Mediterranean diet. Almost four years into keto, I am maintaining my ideal weight, feeling freedom from food like the one I have never had before. Pro Tip: Choose nutrient-packed foods that can satiate you easier, and automatically, you will eat less.

What to Eat on a Ketogenic Diet?

I created a detailed keto-friendly food list so you can keep it in your shopping bag.

Vegetables: Lettuce (all types), greens (spinach, Swiss chard, collard, mustard greens, kale, and turnip); mushrooms, onion, garlic, asparagus, arugula, avocado, celery, squash, kohlrabi, bok choy, radishes, broccoli tomatoes, cauliflower, zucchini, eggplant. In moderation: artichokes, Brussels sprouts, broccolini, cauliflower, cucumbers, green beans, cabbage, okra, snap peas, snow peas, and fennel.

Fruits: Blackberries, cranberries, raspberries, lemon, lime, coconut, and tomatoes.

Meat & Poultry: Beef, pork, game, lamb, and veal, chicken, turkey and duck.

Ground meat: Pork, beef, turkey, and mixed ground meat.

Lunch & Deli Meats: Bacon, pancetta, pepperoni, salami, soppressata, chorizo, ham, pastrami, prosciutto, and speck. In moderation: bologna and mortadella.

Seafood: Fatty fish, white fish, lobster, crab, shrimp, scallops, mussels, squid, oysters, and octopus.

Dairy: Cream cheese, blue cheese, mozzarella, brie, Colby cheese, goat, provolone, Gouda, Muenster, camembert, and Swiss cheese; heavy cream, double cream, half-and-half; butter and ghee; eggs. In moderation: whole milk, cheddar cheese, feta, Pepper Jack cheese, full-fat Greek yogurt, crème fraîche, mascarpone, cottage cheese, sour cream, and ricotta.

Nuts & Seeds: peanuts, almonds, walnuts, Brazil nuts, pecans, hazelnuts, macadamia nuts, pine nuts, chia seeds, hemp seeds, pumpkin seeds, and sunflower seeds.

Fats & Oils: Coconut oil, avocado oil, olive oil, flaxseed oil, cocoa butter, and nut oil; lard, duck fat, schmaltz, and tallow.

Keto-friendly drink options: Coffee, tea, diet soda, seltzer, sparkling water, keto smoothies, zero carb energy drinks.

Other keto-friendly foods include:

Herbs and spices (fresh or dried); bouillon cubes and granules.

Sauces & Condiments: Mayonnaise, mustard, tomato sauce, vinegar, and hot sauce (make sure to check the nutrition facts label).

Canned food: tuna anchovies, crab, salmon, sardines, tomato, sauerkraut, pickles, and olives (make sure to check the nutrition facts label).

Baking ingredients: almond flour, coconut flour, baking powder, baking soda, cocoa, vanilla extract, dark chocolate, glucomannan powder.

Nut & Seed Butters: peanut butter, almond butter, hazelnut butter, macadamia nut butter, coconut butter, pecan butter, sunflower seed butter, walnut butter, and tahini.

Vegetarian: Tempeh, tofu, full-fat coconut milk, jackfruit, nutritional yeast, Shirataki noodles, Nori sheets, roasted seaweed, Kelp noodles, Kelp flakes.

Keto-Friendly Alcohol: Whiskey, brandy, dry martini, vodka, and tequila.

Seaweed: Wakame, chlorella, nori, dulse, spirulina, and kelp.

Keto sweeteners: Stevia drops, Erythritol, and Monkfruit are zero carb sweeteners; Splenda (sucralose-based sweetener) has 0.5g of carbs per packet (1 g); Erythritol has 4 grams of carbs per teaspoon (4 grams); Xylitol has 4 grams of carbs per teaspoon (4 grams);

Foods to Avoid on a Ketogenic Diet

Grains & grain-like seeds: Rice, wheat, quinoa, oats, amaranth, barley, buckwheat, corn, millet

Flours: Wheat flour, cornmeal, arrowroot, cornstarch, cassava, dal, and fava beans.

Starches: Starchy vegetables, soy, lentils, sago, tapioca, plantain, banana, and mesquite.

Sugars: All types of sugar and syrup (rice syrup, malt syrup, sorghum syrup, corn syrup, carob syrup, and high maltose corn syrup), barley malt, cane juice crystals, cane juice, treacle, malt, rapadura, muscovado, panocha, scant, agave nectar, molasses, honey, and maple syrup.

Processed vegetable oils & trans fats: Diglycerides, shortening, vegetable shortening, margarine, interesterified oils, corn oil, cottonseed oil, grapeseed oil, safflower oil, and soybean oil.

Milk & reduced-fat dairy products: evaporated skim milk, low-fat yogurts, fat-free butter substitutes, and reduced fat cheese.

Factory-farmed fish and eggs, processed meat

Fruits (other than berries) & dried fruits

Sugary drinks: soda and energy drinks.

Ketogenic Kitchen Makeover

To make your keto grocery shopping easier, here is the list of pantry essentials on a keto diet. It will help you to save money by not buying unnecessary items.

- LOW-CARB FLOURS – Almond flour (1/4 cup or 28 grams of almond flour has around 160 calories and 6 grams of total carbs); Coconut flour (2 tablespoons or 18 grams of coconut flour has around 45 calories and 11 grams of total carbs); Flax meal (2 tablespoons or 14 grams of flax meal has nearly 70 calories and 5 grams of total carbs); Sunflower seed meal and Pumpkin seed meal.

- SWEETENER – Stevia, Xylitol, Erythritol.

- NUTS & SEEDS

- CREAM CHEESE

- COCONUT MILK & COCONUT CREAM

- COCONUT OIL, AVOCADO OIL & OLIVE OIL

- MEAT, POULTRY & SEAFOOD

- NUT BUTTERS

- KETO VEGETABLES & FROZEN VEGETABLES

- CONDIMENTS – Mustard, mayonnaise, Sriracha, hot sauce, and vinegar.

- CACAO POWDER, CACAO NIBS & SUGAR-FREE DARK CHOCOLATE

- PSYLLIUM HUSKS

- HERBS & SPICES – pink salt, sage, thyme, rosemary, black pepper, oregano, basil, ginger, turmeric, and cinnamon.

CONSIDER MACRONUTRIENT BALANCE

Macronutrients ("macros") include protein, fat, and carbs. Macronutrients provide energy in the form of calories. For instance, fat provides 9 calories per gram; then, there are 4 calories per gram of protein; as for carbohydrates, there are 4 calories per gram. Luckily, you can calculate your keto macros in a couple of minutes by using the Keto Calculator online. It can help you find the exact amount of macronutrients you need to reach your goal, whether you want to lose or maintain your weight. There are calculators for a classic ketogenic diet (75% fat, 20% protein, 5% carbohydrate) and other variations of keto diets so you can input specific amounts of macros according to your preference.

FATS (LIPIDS) are an essential part of a ketogenic diet. The type of fats you eat on a keto diet is essential because some fats are better for weight loss and healthier than others. It took me long to understand that I need to eat fat to burn fat. If you avoid fat and eat large amounts of lean protein foods such as skinless chicken and fish, the excess protein will be converted into glucose. It can raise your insulin levels, too. Low-fat products may seem like a good option for weight loss because fats have been given a bad reputation in the past. However, reduced-fat peanut butter, fat-free salad dressings or low-fat yogurt often contain a lot of unhealthy ingredients, processed oil, and sugar. The trick here is to eat more fat. For example, I'd like to add butter to my breakfast, it fills me up and helps me eat less at lunch. Keep in mind that the human body needs all types of fats including unsaturated fats and saturated fats. There are two main types of unsaturated fats: 1) polyunsaturated fats (include omega-3 fats and omega-6 fats), and 2) monounsaturated fats.

Sources of monounsaturated fatty acids include olive oil, peanut oil, canola oil, sesame oil, and cashews. Foods with a higher amount of polyunsaturated fat include nuts, seeds, soybean oil, and fatty fish. Foods with higher amounts of saturated fats include fatty beef, butter, cheese, pork, poultry with skin, cream, and lard. There is one more category called "Trans fats" that are unsaturated fats that have been processed. You should eat less saturated and trans-fats in order to lower the risk of heart disease, high blood cholesterol, and obesity. To illustrate, junk food and packaged foods contain saturated fat in a larger amount. Therefore, you should avoid snack foods (such as fatty potato chips), fried foods, high fat takeaway foods (including pizza, pasta, hamburgers), high-fat cakes, biscuits, and muffins, pastries (such as pies and croissants). Check the labels and opt for the products that are higher in poly and monounsaturated fats and lower in saturated and trans-fats. Remember, it is important to eat fats in small amounts as a part of a balanced ketogenic diet.

PROTEIN also plays a unique role in the human body. It consists of smaller units called amino acids; you need essential amino acids for your body to function properly. The most important functions of proteins include the creation of hormones, maintaining a healthy weight, promoting longevity, muscle growth and repair. Protein is crucial for a skin, bone, and brain health, too. Animal protein sources on a keto diet include seafood, meat, poultry, cheese, and eggs. Plant protein sources include most nuts and seeds.

There are different views on protein intake on a keto diet. Some ketogenic researchers suggest high protein intake (1 gram of protein per 1 pound). Some experts advocates low protein intake for people who follow a keto diet or 1.0 grams of protein per kilogram of lean mass (2.2 pounds). They believe excess protein can turn into sugar in your body and prevent ketosis. There is the third group of experts that recommends 1.5-1.75 grams of protein per 2.2 pounds. Most people agree that we should follow this formula to enter and stay in ketosis – 5% carbs, 20% protein, and 75% fats.

CARBOHYDRATES are macronutrients that the human body converts to glucose; in fact, glucose is the body's principal fuel source. Your organs such as kidneys, brain, and heart all need carbs to function properly. Furthermore, fats can't be properly metabolized without carbs in the form of fiber that are needed for digestion. Besides being a fuel, glucose can be stored as glycogen in our liver or muscles. Put simply, overconsumption of carbs increases the creation of more fat storage.

The human body also requires micronutrients, including vitamins and minerals. Bear in mind that the majority of micronutrients and important phytonutrients come from vegetables; it means that you should eat a large portion of keto veggies with every meal. When you know your macros, you can easily plan your day on a ketogenic diet.

6 CRITICAL KETOGENIC DIET TIPS

Eat a solid keto breakfast to lose weight.

You should make time to start your day right. Heaving a good breakfast with protein and healthy fats, such as an omelet or egg muffins, will control your eating throughout the day. Eating a healthy low-carb breakfast can significantly restore the glucose levels in your body just like your car needs fuel to run. You should focus on having protein-rich foods such as milk, nuts, seeds, and eggs. Skipping breakfast affects mood and cognitive function. In addition, it may lead to hypertension, high cholesterol, and high blood pressure. Researches have proven that people who skip breakfast have high levels of fatigue throughout the day.

If you think you have no time for breakfast, this recipe collection may help you to overcome that problem. This collection offers easy breakfast ideas such as egg muffins, keto fat bombs, low-carb pancakes, and so forth. You can also turn dinner leftovers into a go-to breakfast. A casserole with eggs and bacon that is topped with sharp cheese makes a fantastic leisure dinner as well as a grab-and-go breakfast. Make-ahead breakfast is good idea for those short on time, too. For instance, you can make lettuce wraps, chicken salad or cheese crisps and store them in airtight containers up to 3 days. You can make a cheese and vegetable gratin in Sunday morning; it can be reheated quickly or enjoyed cold straight from the refrigerator. With our keto recipes, you can easily make meal prep a habit! Remember, your body needs to refuel first thing in the morning. Therefore, take your breakfast within an hour of waking up. Breakfast is an all-important key to a successful keto diet and to better health.

Learn to use the nutrition facts label.

First things first, keep carbs low. It will help you to make better food choices that contribute to your diet. Then, check for hidden sugars, which is "enemy number one" on a keto diet. Most processed foods contain hidden sugar since it enhances flavor and helps preserve foods. Common sweeteners include raw sugar, brown sugar, sucrose, sugar syrup, high-fructose corn syrup, invert sugar, cane sugar, corn syrup, Turbinado, corn sweetener, dextrose, fructose, fruit juice concentrates, maltose, glucose, lactose, malt syrup, and Sorghum syrup. They don't contribute any health benefits to your meals.

You should also avoid the following ingredients: caramel, cane juice, cane juice solids, dextrin, dextran, barley malt, beet sugar, buttered syrup, carob syrup, date sugar, diatase, diatastic malt, golden syrup, Refiner's syrup, and ethyl maltol. Statistics have shown that the average American consumes at least 64 pounds of sugar per year or 22 teaspoons of added sugars a day. When it comes to healthy keto sweeteners, you should opt for a sweetener that is made of natural ingredients and does not contain chemicals. In addition, you should choose a sweetener that has nutritional value but you'll still be within your daily carb limit. Stevia and monk fruit are natural sweeteners that provide health benefits. Stevia is three hundred times sweeter than sugar and has no impact on blood sugar levels. When purchasing stevia, look for a pure, organic product. Monk fruit is a zero-calorie sweetener; studies have proven that monk fruit has significant anti-inflammatory and antioxidant properties. It is useful in reducing inflammation and regulating insulin tolerance.

Learn how to build muscle on a keto diet.

Building lean mass is crucial for a successful ketogenic diet because you will burn off your body's fat storages more efficiently. There are four types of exercises I did for boosting muscle size: Deadlifts, overhead press, squats, and bench press.

It's important to refuel your body with nutrient-dense keto food for optimal athletic performance. In addition, pay close attention to your electrolyte consumption. For example, low-carb, potassium-rich foods include mushrooms, spinach, broccoli, and salmon. Low-carb, magnesium-rich foods include almonds, avocados, and dark chocolate. The body also loses sodium, chloride, and calcium during exercise.

Calculate net carbs.

I know it can be confusing to figure out how much carbs to incorporate into your daily meal plan. Learning how to calculate net carbs is essential for success on a keto diet. In fact, net carbs are the carbohydrates that our body can digest and uses for energy. Stick to the formula: Total Carbohydrate - Dietary Fiber - Sugar Alcohol = Net Carbs. Dietary fiber and sugar alcohol (most of them) are non-digestible carbs. Your liver does not use non-digestible carbs to convert them into glucose. Therefore, net carbs only count starches and sugars.

In other words, you don't need to include sugar alcohols (xylitol, mannitol, lactitol, and erythritol) into your carb limit calculations. On the other hand, each gram of sorbitol, isomalt, maltitol, or glycerin counts as about 0.5 gram of carbs. Further, fiber are all listed under carbs but our body can't process them; they do not have an energy value for the human body. They are generally listed under "Dietary Fiber" on food labels. Soluble dietary fiber plays a key role in the regulation of appetite by achieving stabilized insulin levels. Further, the key to healthy low-carb dieting is to learn about macronutrients and how they affect your body. Thus, you should consider calculating your net carbs rather than total carbs. If you are a beginner, watch out for hidden carbs.

Consider energy density.

In fact, energy density is the number of calories per gram of food. As for a keto diet, it is advisable to base your diet plan around medium energy density foods and eat higher energy density foods in small amounts. On the other hand, lower energy density foods have fewer calories per gram of food. They include clear soups and stews as well as vegetables and simple garden salads that are naturally high in water.

Eat real food.

This means that on a ketogenic diet you'll need to eat whole, unprocessed food that is rich in nutrients. It is extremely important to avoid chemical additives and junk food. Focusing on whole, organic and grass-fed foods will make your life easier and your body healthier.

3 PROVEN BENEFITS OF A KETOGENIC DIET

1) A keto diet leads to weight loss. When you avoid carbohydrates, your body starts burning stored fat; it will automatically cause decreased appetite. On the other hand, you will experience higher energy levels.

3) Mental clarity and better concentration. On a keto diet, our brain uses ketones as the main fuel; consequently, it reduces the levels of toxins. It will significantly improve your cognitive functions, mental focus, concentration, and mental performance.

2) Health benefits. A keto diet restricts carbohydrates; they can be found in unhealthy sugary foods, refined grains such as bread, pasta and white rice. On the other hand, it promotes foods that are loaded with high-quality protein (it is essential for building muscle), good fat, and healthy veggies. Many studies have proven that low-carb diets can significantly improve health. They measured the main outcomes such as LDL cholesterol, HDL cholesterol, blood sugar levels, triglycerides, and weight loss.

Fatty fish such (for example, tuna and salmon) is well known for its ability to lower triglycerides; consequently, it can reduce the risk of stroke. Unsaturated fat-packed foods such as seeds, nuts and unrefined vegetable oils can help your body to lower triglycerides, too. In addition, cutting out carbs can reduce insulin levels and regulate blood sugar. Not only can keto diets improve your physical performance and boost weight loss, but they also treat some serious conditions. Keto diets have proven beneficial in treating several brain disorders such as epilepsy in children. Moreover, ketogenic diets are incredibly effective in treating metabolic syndrome.

A FEW HACKS YOU MIGHT BENEFIT FROM

Stay hydrated – According to the United States National Library of Medicine, an adult person should drink between 2.7 to 3.7 liters of water per day. Be careful of liquid calories on a ketogenic diet. Avoid alcohol and sweetened drinks; you can satisfy your thirst with sparkling water (with added fresh lemon juice), full-fat yogurt, or ice tea. Eat fresh vegetables that are naturally high in water content. As many keto-ers, I experienced dry mouth and bad breath, too; they are common symptoms of ketosis. How I get rid of ketosis breath? The trick is to brush regularly, chew sugar-free gum, and drink more water.

Fat coffee – This is my little secret to burning fat faster. A cup of coffee with a tablespoon of butter gives me a prolonged energy hit until lunchtime. I love its creaminess and distinctly aftertaste and I am impressed by its results. It may sound crazy, but try it once and you will fall in love with "fat black".

Keep it simple – The key to a successful ketogenic diet is making simple tweaks to your lifestyle. Make a simple ketogenic meal plan to get yourself into a routine; stick to easy recipes such as salads and soups. Go for simple snacks, too. Declutter and simplify your kitchen, and choose quick meals to cook at home. Let go of control, relax and go outside. Getting fresh air and spending time with family or pets will help make you more likely to stick to your diet.

3- WEEK MEAL PLAN

I created an easy-to-follow meal plan for you to kick-start your keto journey right. This is a sample menu for three weeks on a ketogenic diet plan.

DAY 1

Breakfast – 1 tablespoon of peanut butter; 1 slice of keto bread

Lunch – Easy Turkey Curry; 1 handful of iceberg lettuce

Dinner – Smoked Haddock Fish Burgers; 1 medium tomato

DAY 2

Breakfast – 1 hard-boiled egg; 1 slice of bacon; 1 shake with 1/2 cup of coconut milk and protein powder

Lunch – Classic Beef Stroganoff; 1 serving of cauliflower rice

Dinner – Alaskan Cod with Mustard Cream Sauce; 1 medium tomato

DAY 3

Breakfast – Paprika Omelet with Goat Cheese; 5-6 almonds

Lunch – Chinese Ground Beef Skillet; 1 cup raw baby spinach with apple cider vinegar

Dinner – Special Chicken Salad; 1 keto dinner roll

DAY 4

Breakfast – Omelet with veggies; 1 slice of bacon

Lunch – Pork Cutlets in Chili Tangy Sauce; 1 serving of coleslaw

Dinner – Lemon Garlic Grilled Chicken Wings; 1 medium tomato

DAY 5

Breakfast – Dilly Boiled Eggs with Avocado; a dollop of sour cream; 1-2 pickles

Lunch – Beef Shredded Beef with Herbs; 1 handful of mixed green salad with a few drizzles of a freshly squeezed lemon juice

Dinner – Two-Cheese Zucchini Gratin; 1 teaspoon of mustard

DAY 6

Breakfast – Greek-Style Frittata with Herbs; 1 keto roll

Lunch – Holiday Pork Belly with Vegetables; 1 serving of cauliflower rice

Dinner – Ranch and Blue Cheese Dip; Greek-style salad (tomato, cucumber, bell peppers, feta cheese)

DAY 7

Breakfast – Mangalorean Egg Curry

Lunch – Italian Zuppa di Pomodoro; 1 large tomato; 1 cup of fried mushrooms with 1 tablespoon of butter

Dinner – Ranch Chicken Wings; Cheese and Artichoke Dip

DAY 8

Breakfast – Scrambled eggs; 1 tomato; 1/2 cup of Greek-style yogurt

Lunch – Cheeseburger Skillet with Bacon and Mushrooms; 1 serving of cauliflower rice

Dinner – Swedish Herring Salad

DAY 9

Breakfast – Egg, Bacon and Kale Muffins; 1/2 cup unsweetened almond milk

Lunch – Hearty Fisherman's Stew; 1 serving of cabbage salad

Dinner – Two-Cheese and Kale Bake

DAY 10

Breakfast – Cauliflower, Cheese and Egg Fat Bombs

Lunch – Grandma's Zucchini and Spinach Chowder; 1/2 chicken breast; 1 scallion

Dinner – Italian Cheese Crisps; a dollop of sour cream; 2 tablespoons tomato paste

DAY 11

Breakfast – 1 tablespoon of peanut butter; 1 slice of keto bread

Lunch – Country-Style Pork Stew; 1 serving of cabbage salad

Dinner – Cauliflower, Ham and Cheese Bake

DAY 12

Breakfast – The Best Zucchini Fritters Ever; 1/2 cup of full-fat Greek yogurt

Lunch – Filipino Nilaga Soup; 1 serving of low-carb grilled vegetables

Dinner – Peanut Butter Cubes

DAY 13

Breakfast – Crêpes with Peanut Butter and Coconut

Lunch – Creamy Broccoli and Bacon Soup; 1 medium cucumber; 1 roasted chicken drumstick

Dinner – Mexican-Style Pork Tacos

DAY 14

Breakfast – Vanilla Mug Cake

Lunch – Cheesy Zucchini Casserole; 1 handful of baby spinach with 1 teaspoon of mustard and 1 teaspoon of olive oil

Dinner – Turkey Crust Pizza with Bacon

DAY 15

Breakfast – Easiest Brownies Ever

Lunch – Salmon Curry with a Twist; 1 serving of roasted keto veggies

Dinner – Stuffed Spaghetti Squash Bowls

DAY 16

Breakfast – Deviled Eggs with Mustard and Chives; 1/2 cup of Greek-style yogurt

Lunch – Ranch Chicken Breasts with Cheese

Dinner – Spicy Baked Eggplant with Herbs and Cheese; Almond Butter and Chocolate Cookies

DAY 17

Breakfast – 2 hard-boiled eggs; 2 slices of Cheddar cheese

Lunch – Pork Tenderloin with Southern Cabbage; 1 slice of keto bread

Dinner – Italian-Style Spicy Meatballs; 1 cucumber

DAY 18

Breakfast – Lettuce Wraps with Ham and Cheese

Lunch – Stuffed Peppers with Cauliflower and Cheese; 1/2 grilled chicken breast

Dinner – Smoked Haddock Fish Burgers

DAY 19

Breakfast – Double Cheese and Sausage Balls

Lunch – Indian-Style Fried Pork; 1 serving of steamed broccoli; 1 cucumber

Dinner – 1 grilled pork sausage; 1 teaspoon Dijon mustard; Chinese-Style Cauliflower Rice

DAY 20

Breakfast – Cheesy Brussels Sprouts; 1 medium tomato with 2-3 Kalamata olives

Lunch – Spinach with Paprika and Cheese; 1 dollop of sour cream

Dinner – Rich Double-Cheese Meatloaf

DAY 21

Breakfast – Mini Stuffed Peppers; 1 serving of blue cheese

Lunch – Holiday Pork Belly with Vegetables; 1 serving of cabbage salad

Dinner – 1 steamed chicken breast; 1 serving of roasted asparagus; Peanut Butter and Chocolate Treat

If you get hungry between meals, there are healthy, keto snacks that can fill you up. They include one or two hard-boiled eggs, baby carrots with tablespoon or two of a keto dipping sauce, full-fat yogurt with tablespoon or two of fresh berries, a handful of nuts, and a few cheese sticks.

ALL ABOUT OUR RECIPE COLLECTION

My goal with this book is to support and inspire people who decide to make a positive change in their lives. For that reason, this book features 75 recipes, from simple recipes for new keto-ers to festive recipes that everyone will love, so that you never run out of ideas.

All of these recipes are made with common ingredients that deliver great flavor and stunning aromas. They are approved by my husband and my guests who often come over for dinner. They are designed to guide you every step of the way in order to prepare the best keto foods ever. Each recipe includes the nutritional information and has up to 6 grams of net carbs. This is the best way to track your macronutrients and customize your diet to fit your unique needs. Besides being a great source for keto recipes, the book is chock-full of cooking secrets, crafty tricks, and handy hacks. Are you ready to go keto? Go ahead! Remember, if I can do it, you can too!

VEGETABLES & SIDE DISHES

1. Cauliflower, Ham and Cheese Bake

This creamy casserole tastes so divine! Cauliflower combines beautifully with ham, cheese, Greek-yogurt and Mediterranean herbs.

Servings 4

Ready in about 40 minutes

NUTRITIONAL INFORMATION (Per serving)

188 - Calories
11.3g - Fat
5.7g - Carbs
1.1g - Fiber
14.9g - Protein
2.9g - Sugars

Ingredients

- 1/2 teaspoon butter, melted
- 1 (1/2-pound) head cauliflower, broken into florets
- 1/2 cup Swiss cheese, shredded
- 1/2 cup Mexican blend cheese, room temperature
- 1/2 cup Greek-style yogurt
- 1 cup cooked ham, chopped
- 1 roasted chili pepper, chopped
- 1/2 teaspoon porcini powder
- 1 teaspoon garlic powder
- 1 teaspoon shallot powder
- 1/2 teaspoon cayenne pepper
- 1/4 teaspoon dried sage
- 1/2 teaspoon dried oregano
- Sea salt and ground black pepper, to taste

Directions

1. Start by preheating your oven to 340 degrees F. Then, coat the bottom and sides of a casserole dish with 1/2 teaspoon of melted butter.
2. Empty the cauliflower into a pot and cover it with water. Let it cook for 6 minutes until it is nice and tender (mashable). Mash the prepared cauliflower with a potato ricer press or potato masher.
3. Now, stir in the cheese; stir until the cheese has melted. Add Greek-style yogurt, chopped ham, roasted pepper, and spices.
4. Place the mixture in the prepared casserole dish; bake in the preheated oven for 20 minutes. Let it sit for about 10 minutes before cutting. Serve and enjoy!

2. Creamy Broccoli and Bacon Soup

This creamy soup will help you keep your diet on track. It can be refrigerated up to 3 days.

Servings 4

Ready in about 20 minutes

NUTRITIONAL INFORMATION (Per serving)

95 - Calories
7.6g - Fat
4.1g - Carbs
1g - Fiber
3g - Protein
1.7g - Sugars

Ingredients

- 2 slices bacon, chopped
- 2 tablespoons scallions, chopped
- 1 carrot, chopped
- 1 celery, chopped
- Salt and ground black pepper, to taste
- 1 teaspoon garlic, finely chopped
- 1/2 teaspoon dried rosemary
- 1 sprig thyme, stripped and chopped
- 1/2 head green cabbage, shredded
- 1/2 head broccoli, broken into small florets
- 3 cups water
- 1 cup chicken stock
- 1/2 cup full-fat yogurt

Directions

1. Heat a stockpot over medium heat; now, sear the bacon until crisp. Reserve the bacon and 1 tablespoon of fat.
2. Then, cook scallions, carrots, and celery in 1 tablespoon of reserved fat. Add salt, pepper, and garlic; cook an additional 1 minute or until fragrant.
3. Now, stir in rosemary, thyme, cabbage, and broccoli. Pour in water and stock, bringing to a rapid boil; reduce heat and let it simmer for 10 minutes more.
4. Add yogurt and cook an additional 5 minutes, stirring occasionally. Use an immersion blender, to puree your soup until smooth.
5. Taste and adjust the seasonings. Garnish with the cooked bacon just before serving.

3. Spinach with Paprika and Cheese

Make a popular side dish in 10 minutes and amaze your guests! Other common additions to this recipe include Parmesan cheese, nutmeg and herbs.

Servings 4

Ready in about 10 minutes

NUTRITIONAL INFORMATION (Per serving)

166 - Calories
15.1g - Fat
5g - Carbs
1.7g - Fiber
4.4g - Protein
2.1g - Sugars

Ingredients

- 1 tablespoon butter, room temperature
- 1 clove garlic, minced
- 10 ounces spinach
- 1/2 teaspoon garlic salt
- 1/4 teaspoon ground black pepper, or more to taste
- 1/2 teaspoon cayenne pepper
- 3 ounces cream cheese
- 1/2 cup double cream

Directions

1. Melt the butter in a saucepan that is preheated over medium heat. Once hot. Cook garlic for 30 seconds.
2. Now, add the spinach; cover the pan for 2 minutes to let the spinach wilt. Season with salt, black pepper, and cayenne pepper
3. Stir in cheese and cream; stir until the cheese melts. Serve immediately.

4. Cheesy Zucchini Casserole

This is a great way to use up the bounty of zucchini during the summer season. You're going to love this easy cheese casserole!

Servings 4

Ready in about 50 minutes

NUTRITIONAL INFORMATION (Per serving)

155 - Calories
12.9g - Fat
3.5g - Carbs
0.8g - Fiber
7.6g - Protein
0.2g - Sugars

Ingredients

- Nonstick cooking spray
- 2 cups zucchini, thinly sliced
- 2 tablespoons leeks, sliced
- 1/2 teaspoon salt
- Freshly ground black pepper, to taste
- 1/2 teaspoon dried basil
- 1/2 teaspoon dried oregano
- 1/2 cup Cheddar cheese, grated
- 1/4 cup heavy cream
- 4 tablespoons Parmesan cheese, freshly grated
- 1 tablespoon butter, room temperature
- 1 teaspoon fresh garlic, minced

Directions

1. Start by preheating your oven to 370 degrees F. Lightly grease a casserole dish with a nonstick cooking spray.
2. Place 1 cup of the zucchini slices in the dish; add 1 tablespoon of leeks; sprinkle with salt, pepper, basil, and oregano. Top with 1/4 cup of Cheddar cheese. Repeat the layers one more time.
3. In a mixing dish, thoroughly whisk the heavy cream with Parmesan, butter, and garlic. Spread this mixture over the zucchini layer and cheese layers.
4. Place in the preheated oven and bake for about 40 to 45 minutes until the edges are nicely browned. Sprinkle with chopped chives, if desired. Bon appétit!

5. Stuffed Peppers with Cauliflower and Cheese

Above ground vegetables such as bell pepper and cauliflower are generally good keto options while below ground vegetables contain more carbs. These peppers are delicious served hot or cold. Enjoy!

Servings 6

Ready in about 45 minutes

NUTRITIONAL INFORMATION (Per serving)

244 - Calories
12.9g - Fat
3.2g - Carbs
1g - Fiber
16.5g - Protein
1.6g - Sugars

Ingredients

- 2 tablespoons vegetable oil
- 2 tablespoons yellow onion, chopped
- 1 teaspoon fresh garlic, crushed
- 1/2 pound ground pork
- 1/2 pound ground turkey
- 1 cup cauliflower rice
- 1/2 teaspoon sea salt
- 1/4 teaspoon red pepper flakes, crushed
- 1/2 teaspoon ground black pepper
- 1 teaspoon dried parsley flakes
- 6 medium-sized bell peppers, deveined and cleaned
- 1/2 cup tomato sauce
- 1/2 cup Cheddar cheese, shredded

Directions

1. Heat the oil in a pan over medium flame. Once hot, sauté the onion and garlic for 2 to 3 minutes.
2. Add the ground meat and cook for 6 minutes longer or until it is nicely browned. Add cauliflower rice and seasoning. Continue to cook for a further 3 minutes.
3. Divide the filling between the prepared bell peppers. Cover with a piece of foil. Place the peppers in a baking pan; add tomato sauce.
4. Bake in the preheated oven at 380 degrees F for 20 minutes. Uncover, top with cheese, and bake for 10 minutes more. Bon appétit!

6. Chinese-Style Cauliflower Rice

This Asian-style omelet with cauliflower is full of healthy keto foods. You can add some chilli for an extra kick, if desired.

Servings 3

Ready in about 15 minutes

NUTRITIONAL INFORMATION (Per serving)

131 - Calories
8.9g - Fat
6.2g - Carbs
1.8g - Fiber
7.2g - Protein
2.2g - Sugars

Ingredients

- 1/2 pound fresh cauliflower
- 1 tablespoon sesame oil
- 1/2 cup leeks, chopped
- 1 garlic, pressed
- Sea salt and freshly ground black pepper, to taste
- 1/2 teaspoon Chinese five-spice powder
- 1 teaspoon oyster sauce
- 1/2 teaspoon light soy sauce
- 1 tablespoon Shaoxing wine
- 3 eggs

Directions

1. Pulse the cauliflower in a food processor until it resembles rice.
2. Heat the sesame oil in a pan over medium-high heat; sauté the leeks and garlic for 2 to 3 minutes. Add the prepared cauliflower rice to the pan, along with salt, black pepper, and Chinese five-spice powder.
3. Next, add oyster sauce, soy sauce, and wine. Let it cook, stirring occasionally, until the cauliflower is crisp-tender, about 5 minutes.
4. Then, add the eggs to the pan; stir until everything is well combined. Serve warm and enjoy!

7. Spicy Baked Eggplant with Herbs and Cheese

Eggplant is baked between layers of Italian cheese, kale, and garlic-tomato pasta sauce, making this Italian-inspired meal oh-so-delicious! You can add a few sprinkles of other Italian spices such as parsley and sage, if desired. You can also garnish your dish with fresh herbs for an extra flavor and even better presentation.

Servings 6

Ready in about
2 hours
45 minutes

NUTRITIONAL
INFORMATION
(Per serving)

230 - Calories
18.5g - Fat
6.7g - Carbs
2.4g - Fiber
10.6g - Protein
3.3g - Sugars

Ingredients

- 1 (3/4-pound) eggplant, cut into 1/2-inch slices
- 1 tablespoon olive oil
- 1 tablespoon butter, melted
- 8 ounces kale leaves, torn into pieces
- 14 ounces garlic-and-tomato pasta sauce, without sugar
- 1/3 cup cream cheese
- 1 cup Asiago cheese, shredded
- 1/2 cup Gorgonzola cheese, grated
- 2 tablespoons ketchup, without sugar
- 1 teaspoon Peperoncino (hot pepper)
- 1 teaspoon Basilico (basil)
- 1 teaspoon oregano
- 1/2 teaspoon Rosmarino (rosemary)

Directions

1. Place the eggplant slices in a colander and sprinkle them with salt. Allow it to sit for 2 hours. Wipe the eggplant slices with paper towels.
2. Brush the eggplant slices with olive oil; cook in a cast-iron grill pan until nicely browned on both sides, about 5 minutes.
3. Melt the butter in a pan over medium flame. Now, cook the kale leaves until wilted. In a mixing bowl, combine the three types of cheese.
4. Transfer the grilled eggplant slices to a lightly greased baking dish. Top with the kale. Then, add a layer of 1/2 of cheese blend.
5. Pour the tomato sauce over the cheese layer. Top with the remaining cheese mixture. Sprinkle with seasoning.
6. Bake in the preheated oven at 350 degrees F until cheese is bubbling and golden brown, about 35 minutes. Bon appétit!

8. The Best Zucchini Fritters Ever

These fritters are quick and easy to whip up for dinner. Serve with a dollop of sour cream, if desired. You can serve them as a side, too.

Servings 6

Ready in about 40 minutes

NUTRITIONAL INFORMATION (Per serving)

111 - Calories
8.9g - Fat
3.2g - Carbs
1g - Fiber
5.8g - Protein
0.5g - Sugars

Ingredients

- 1 pound zucchini, grated and drained
- 1 egg
- 1 teaspoon fresh Italian parsley
- 1/2 cup almond meal
- 1/2 cup goat cheese, crumbled
- Sea salt and ground black pepper, to taste
- 1/2 teaspoon red pepper flakes, crushed
- 2 tablespoons olive oil

Directions

1. Mix all ingredients, except for the olive oil, in a large bowl. Let it sit in your refrigerator for 30 minutes.
2. Heat the oil into a non-stick frying pan over medium heat; scoop the heaped tablespoons of the zucchini mixture into the hot oil.
3. Cook for 3 to 4 minutes; then, gently flip the fritters over and cook on the other side. Cook in a couple of batches.
4. Transfer to a paper towel to soak up any excess grease. Serve and enjoy!

9. Stuffed Spaghetti Squash Bowls

All the flavors of your favorite pasta are packed into these edible bowls, but they are keto-friendly and guilt-free! These bowls look really fancy, they are suitable for any occasion.

Servings 4

Ready in about 1 hour

NUTRITIONAL INFORMATION
(Per serving)

219 Calories
17.5g - Fat
6.9g - Carbs
0.9g - Fiber
9g - Protein
4.1g - Sugars

Ingredients

- 1/2 pound spaghetti squash, halved, scoop out seeds
- 1 teaspoon olive oil
- 1/2 cup Mozzarella cheese, shredded
- 1/2 cup cream cheese
- 1/2 cup full-fat Greek yogurt
- 2 eggs
- 1 garlic clove, minced
- 1/2 teaspoon cumin
- 1/2 teaspoon basil
- 1/2 teaspoon mint
- Sea salt and ground black pepper, to taste

Directions

1. Place the squash halves in a baking pan; drizzle the insides of each squash half with olive oil.
2. Bake in the preheated oven at 370 degrees F for 45 to 50 minutes or until the interiors are easily pierced through with a fork
3. Now, scrape out the spaghetti squash "noodles" from the skin in a mixing bowl. Add the remaining ingredients and mix to combine well.
4. Carefully fill each of the squash half with the cheese mixture. Bake at 350 degrees F for 5 to 10 minutes, until the cheese is bubbling and golden brown. Bon appétit!

POULTRY

10. Tangy Classic Chicken Drumettes

A ketogenic dinner doesn't have to be complicated. Simple ingredients –
chicken, lemon, garlic. Minimal work—maximum pay-off!

Servings 4

Ready in about 40 minutes

NUTRITIONAL INFORMATION (Per serving)

209 - Calories
12.2g - Fat
0.4g - Carbs
0.1g - Fiber
23.2g - Protein
0.1g - Sugars

Ingredients

- 1 pound chicken drumettes
- 1 tablespoon olive oil
- 2 tablespoons butter, melted
- 1 garlic cloves, sliced
- Fresh juice of 1/2 lemon
- 2 tablespoons white wine
- Salt and ground black pepper, to taste
- 1 tablespoon fresh scallions, chopped

Directions

1. Start by preheating your oven to 440 degrees F. Place the chicken in a parchment-lined baking pan. Drizzle with olive oil and melted butter.
2. Add the garlic, lemon, wine, salt, and black pepper.
3. Bake in the preheated oven for about 35 minutes. Serve garnished with fresh scallions. Enjoy!

11. Easy Turkey Curry

Ginger powder is loaded with health benefits, while a curry paste makes your food tastes so good. You can also add herbed salt, paprika, chives, and other spice blends.

Servings 4

Ready in about 1 hour

NUTRITIONAL INFORMATION (Per serving)

295 - Calories
19.5g - Fat
2.9g - Carbs
0g - Fiber
25.5g - Protein
3.1g - Sugars

Ingredients

- 3 teaspoons sesame oil
- 1 pound turkey wings, boneless and chopped
- 2 cloves garlic, finely chopped
- 1 small-sized red chili pepper, minced
- 1/2 teaspoon turmeric powder
- 1/2 teaspoon ginger powder
- 1 teaspoon red curry paste
- 1 cup unsweetened coconut milk, preferably homemade
- 1/2 cup water
- 1/2 cup turkey consommé
- Kosher salt and ground black pepper, to taste

Directions

1. Heat sesame oil in a sauté pan. Add the turkey and cook until it is light brown about 7 minutes.
2. Add garlic, chili pepper, turmeric powder, ginger powder, and curry paste and cook for 3 minutes longer.
3. Add the milk, water, and consommé. Season with salt and black pepper. Cook for 45 minutes over medium heat. Bon appétit!

12. Ranch Chicken Breasts with Cheese

Servings 4

Ready in about 20 minutes

NUTRITIONAL INFORMATION (Per serving)

295 - Calories
19.5g - Fat
2.9g - Carbs
0g - Fiber
25.5g - Protein
3.1g - Sugars

Ingredients

- 2 chicken breasts
- 2 tablespoons butter, melted
- 1 teaspoon salt
- 1/2 teaspoon garlic powder
- 1/2 teaspoon cayenne pepper
- 1/2 teaspoon black peppercorns, crushed
- 1/2 tablespoon ranch seasoning mix
- 4 ounces Ricotta cheese, room temperature
- 1/2 cup Monterey-Jack cheese, grated
- 4 slices bacon, chopped
- 1/4 cup scallions, chopped

Directions

1. Start by preheating your oven to 370 degrees F.
2. Drizzle the chicken with melted butter. Rub the chicken with salt, garlic powder, cayenne pepper, black pepper, and ranch seasoning mix.
3. Heat a cast iron skillet over medium heat. Cook the chicken for 3 to 5 minutes per side. Transfer the chicken to a lightly greased baking dish.
4. Add cheese and bacon. Bake about 12 minutes. Top with scallions just before serving. Bon appétit!

13. Cheesy Chicken Drumsticks

Chicken, spices, lots of cheese... what's not to love about these low-carb, creamy drumsticks? Peanut oil has a high smoke point; you can use unrefined sunflower oil and avocado oil, too.

Servings 2

Ready in about

NUTRITIONAL INFORMATION (Per serving)

589 - Calories
46g - Fat
5.8g - Carbs
1g - Fiber
37.5g - Protein
3.8g - Sugars

Ingredients

- 1 tablespoon peanut oil
- 2 chicken drumsticks
- 1/2 cup vegetable broth
- 1/2 cup cream cheese
- 2 cups baby spinach
- Sea salt and ground black pepper, to taste
- 1/2 teaspoon parsley flakes
- 1/2 teaspoon shallot powder
- 1/2 teaspoon garlic powder
- 1/2 cup Asiago cheese, grated

Directions

1. Heat the oil in a pan over medium-high heat. Then cook the chicken for 7 minutes, turning occasionally; reserve.
2. Pour in broth; add cream cheese and spinach; cook until spinach has wilted. Add the chicken back to the pan.
3. Add seasonings and Asiago cheese; cook until everything is thoroughly heated, an additional 4 minutes. Serve immediately and enjoy!

14. Special Chicken Salad

You can add boiled eggs to the salad just like grandma used to make. You can also use leftover chicken from a roast chicken.

Servings 3

**Ready in about
1 hour
20 minutes**

**NUTRITIONAL
INFORMATION
(Per serving)**

400 - Calories
35.1g - Fat
5.6g - Carbs
2.9g - Fiber
16.1g - Protein
2.2g - Sugars

Ingredients

- 1 chicken breast, skinless
- 1/4 mayonnaise
- 1/4 cup sour cream
- 2 tablespoons Cottage cheese, room temperature
- Salt and black pepper, to taste
- 1/4 cup sunflower seeds, hulled and roasted
- 1/2 avocado, peeled and cubed
- 1/2 teaspoon fresh garlic, minced
- 2 tablespoons scallions, chopped

Directions

1. Bring a pot of well-salted water to a rolling boil.
2. Add the chicken to the boiling water; now, turn off the heat, cover, and let the chicken stand in the hot water for 15 minutes.
3. Then, drain the water; chop the chicken into bite-sized pieces. Add the remaining ingredients and mix well.
4. Place in the refrigerator for at least one hour. Serve well chilled. Enjoy!

15. Turkey Crust Pizza with Bacon

This delicious low-carb pizza is much better than takeout. Other topping ideas include pepperoni, spinach, onion, and marinara sauce. Enjoy!

Servings 4

Ready in about 35 minutes

NUTRITIONAL INFORMATION (Per serving)

360 - Calories
22.7g - Fat
5.9g - Carbs
0.7g - Fiber
32.6g - Protein
2.7g - Sugars

Ingredients

- 1/2 pound ground turkey
- 1/2 cup Parmesan cheese, freshly grated
- 1/2 cup Mozzarella cheese, grated
- Salt and ground black pepper, to taste
- 1 bell pepper, sliced
- 2 slices Canadian bacon, chopped
- 1 tomato, chopped
- 1 teaspoon oregano
- 1/2 teaspoon basil

Directions

1. In mixing bowl, thoroughly combine the ground turkey, cheese, salt, and black pepper.
2. Then, press the cheese-chicken mixture into a parchment-lined baking pan. Bake in the preheated oven, at 390 degrees F for 22 minutes.
3. Add bell pepper, bacon, tomato, oregano, and basil. Bake an additional 10 minutes and serve warm. Bon appétit!

16. Old-Fashioned Chicken Soup

This no-noodle chicken soup is hearty and delicious when it's cold outside.
It will be a huge hit during the winter season!

Servings 6

**Ready in about
55 minutes**

**NUTRITIONAL
INFORMATION
(Per serving)**

265 - Calories
23.8g - Fat
4.3g - Carbs
1.7g - Fiber
9.3g - Protein
2.3g - Sugars

Ingredients

- 1 rotisserie chicken, shredded
- 6 cups water
- 2 tablespoons butter
- 2 celery stalks, chopped
- 1/2 onion, chopped
- 1 bay leaf
- Sea salt and ground black pepper, to taste
- 1 tablespoon fresh cilantro, chopped
- 2 cups green cabbage, sliced into strips

Directions

1. Cook the bones and carcass from a leftover chicken with water over medium-high heat for 15 minutes. Then, reduce to a simmer and cook an additional 15 minutes. Reserve the chicken along with the broth.
2. Let it cool enough to handle, shred the meat into bite-size pieces.
3. Melt the butter in a large stockpot over medium heat. Sauté the celery and onion until tender and fragrant.
4. Add bay leaf, salt, pepper, and broth, and let it simmer for 10 minutes.
5. Add the reserved chicken, cilantro, and cabbage. Simmer for an additional 10 to 11 minutes, until the cabbage is tender. Bon appétit!

17. Crispy Chicken Filets in Tomato Sauce

The key to this recipe is to crush the pork rinds in a Ziploc bag by hand, since we need a panko-like texture. A simple tomato sauce goes along very well with chicken.

Servings 3

Ready in about 15 minutes

NUTRITIONAL INFORMATION
(Per serving)

359 - Calories
23.6g - Fat
5.8g - Carbs
1.2g - Fiber
30.4g - Protein
3.1g - Sugars

Ingredients

- 2 tablespoons double cream
- 1 egg
- 2 ounces pork rinds, crushed
- 2 ounces Romano cheese, grated
- Sea salt and ground black pepper, to taste
- 1 teaspoon cayenne pepper
- 1 teaspoon dried parsley
- 1 garlic clove, halved
- 1/2 pound chicken fillets
- 2 tablespoons olive oil
- 1 large-sized Roma tomato, pureed

Directions

1. In a mixing bowl, whisk the cream and egg.
2. In another bowl, mix the crushed pork rinds, Romano cheese, salt, black pepper, cayenne pepper, and dried parsley.
3. Rub the garlic halves all over the chicken. Dip the chicken fillets into the egg mixture; then, coat the chicken with breading on all sides.
4. Heat the olive oil in a pan over medium-high heat; add ghee. Once hot, cook chicken fillets until no longer pink, 2 to 4 minutes on each side.
5. Transfer the prepared chicken fillets to a baking pan that is lightly greased with a nonstick cooking spray. Cover with the pureed tomato. Bake for 2 to 3 minutes until everything is thoroughly warmed. Bon appétit!

18. Lemon Garlic Grilled Chicken Wings

For a quick dinner on busy weeknights, place some chicken wings and marinade in a Ziploc bag; freeze them and Voila! On an actual day, thaw them and place on the preheated grill.

Servings 4

Ready in about 25 minutes + marinating time

NUTRITIONAL INFORMATION (Per serving)

131 - Calories
7.8g - Fat
1.8g - Carbs
0.2g - Fiber
13.4g - Protein
0.4g - Sugars

Ingredients

- 8 chicken wings
- 2 tablespoons ghee, melted
- The Marinade:
- 2 garlic cloves, minced
- 1/4 cup leeks, chopped
- 2 tablespoons lemon juice
- Salt and ground black pepper, to taste
- 1/2 teaspoon paprika
- 1 teaspoon dried rosemary

Directions

1. Thoroughly combine all ingredients for the marinade in a ceramic bowl. Add the chicken wings to the bowl.
2. Cover and allow it to marinate for 1 hour.
3. Then, preheat your grill to medium-high heat. Drizzle melted ghee over the chicken wings. Grill the chicken wings for 20 minutes, turning them periodically.
4. Taste, adjust the seasonings, and serve warm. Enjoy!

PORK

19. Mexican-Style Pork Tacos

You could serve this pork mixture on a bed of zucchini noodles. Other popular fixings include shredded cheese, guacamole, Tabasco sauce, mustard, tomato, and bell peppers.

Servings 4

Ready in about 20 minutes

NUTRITIONAL INFORMATION (Per serving)

330 - Calories
26.3g - Fat
4.9g - Carbs
1.3g - Fiber
17.9g - Protein
2.4g - Sugars

Ingredients

- 6 ounces ground pork
- 4 ounces ground turkey
- Sea salt and ground black pepper, to taste
- 1 tablespoon lard
- 4 tablespoons roasted tomatillo salsa
- 12 lettuce leaves
- 4 tablespoons fresh cilantro, chopped
- 4 tablespoons sour cream

Directions

1. In a mixing bowl, thoroughly combine the ground pork, turkey, salt, and black pepper.
2. Melt the lard in a skillet over medium-high heat. Once hot, cook the meat mixture for 5 to 6 minutes, crumbling with a fork.
3. Add the roasted tomatillo salsa and stir to combine well.
4. To assemble the tacos, divide the salsa-meat mixture between lettuce leaves. Top with cilantro and sour cream. Make wraps and serve immediately.

20. Pork Cutlets in Chili Tangy Sauce

These pork cutlets are perfectly seasoned and cooked with lots of herbs.
Finally, they are served with a spicy sherry sauce.

Servings 4

**Ready in about
15 minutes**

**NUTRITIONAL
INFORMATION
(Per serving)**

288 - Calories
17.3g - Fat
1.1g - Carbs
0g - Fiber
29.9g - Protein
0.1g - Sugars

Ingredients

- 1 pound pork cutlets
- Sea salt and ground black pepper, to taste
- 1/2 teaspoon thyme
- 1/2 teaspoon rosemary
- 1 teaspoon basil
- 1 tablespoon lard, room temperature

The Sauce:
- 2 tablespoons sherry
- 1/4 cup sour cream
- 1/4 cup beef bone broth
- 1 teaspoon mustard
- 1/2 teaspoon turmeric powder
- 1/2 teaspoon chili powder

Directions

1. Season the pork cutlets with salt, pepper, thyme, rosemary, and basil.
2. Melt the lard in a pan over medium-high heat; now, sear pork cutlets for 3 minutes; turn them over and cook for 3 minutes on the other side. Reserve.
3. Deglaze your pan with sherry; now, add the remaining ingredients and cook on medium-low heat until the sauce has thickened slightly.
4. Add the reserved pork and let it simmer for a couple of minutes or until everything is heated through. Spoon the sauce over pork cutlets and serve.

21. Holiday Pork Belly with Vegetables

Are you thinking about an oven roasted crispy pork? Look no further! This pork belly is tender with amazing crispy skin.

Servings 4

Ready in about 20 minutes

NUTRITIONAL
INFORMATION
(Per serving)

607 - Calories
60g - Fat
4.4g - Carbs
0.7g - Fiber
11.4g - Protein
2.1g - Sugars

Ingredients

- 1 pound skinless pork belly
- Himalayan salt and freshly ground black pepper, to taste
- 1 teaspoon dried parsley
- 1 teaspoon dried basil
- 1/2 teaspoon dried oregano
- 2 cloves garlic, pressed
- 1/2 cup shallots, sliced
- 1 red bell pepper, seeded and sliced
- 1 green bell pepper, seeded and sliced

Directions

1. Poke holes all over the pork with a fork. Rub the seasonings all over the pork belly. Place the pork in a lightly greased baking pan.
2. Top with garlic, shallots, and peppers. Transfer the pork belly to the preheated oven.
3. Bake at 390 degrees F for about 18 minutes. Serve warm.

22. Cheeseburger Skillet with Bacon and Mushrooms

Are you craving cheeseburgers but you do not have the time to cook them? No worries, this amazing dish comes together in one skillet in less than 20 minutes.

Servings 4

Ready in about

NUTRITIONAL INFORMATION (Per serving)

463 - Calories
60g - Fat
4.7g - Carbs
0.8g - Fiber
36.2g - Protein
3g - Sugars

Ingredients

- 2 slices Canadian bacon, chopped
- 1/2 cup shallots, sliced
- 1 garlic clove, minced
- 1 pound ground pork
- Sea salt and ground black pepper, to taste
- 1/3 cup vegetable broth
- 1/4 cup white wine
- 6 ounces Cremini mushrooms, sliced
- 1/2 cup cream cheese

Directions

1. Heat a cast-iron skillet over medium heat. Cook the bacon for 2 to 3 minutes; reserve the bacon and 1 tablespoon of fat. Then, sauté the shallots and garlic in 1 tablespoon of bacon fat until tender and fragrant.
2. Add the ground pork, salt, and black pepper to the skillet. Cook for 4 to 5 minutes or until ground meat is nicely browned.
3. Add broth, wine, and mushrooms. Cover and cook for 8 to 9 minutes over medium flame.
4. Turn off the heat. Add cream cheese and stir to combine. Serve topped with the reserved bacon. Enjoy!

23. Country-Style Pork Stew

Servings 4

Ready in about 40 minutes

NUTRITIONAL INFORMATION (Per serving)

351 - Calories
22.7g - Fat
2.7g - Carbs
0.5g - Fiber
32.3g - Protein
1.5g - Sugars

Ingredients

- 2 tablespoons lard, room temperature
- 1/4 cup leeks, chopped
- 2 garlic cloves, minced
- 1 (1-inch) piece ginger root, peeled and chopped
- 1 bell pepper, seeded and chopped
- 1 pound pork stew meat, cubed
- 1/2 cup tomato paste
- 2 cups chicken broth
- Sea salt and ground black pepper, to taste
- 1 teaspoon paprika
- 1 bay leaf
- 1/4 cup Creme fraiche

Directions

1. Melt the lard in a sauté pan that is preheated over medium heat. Then, cook the leeks, garlic, and ginger until aromatic, about 3 minutes.
2. Add bell pepper and cook for a further 2 minutes, stirring periodically. Add the pork and cook an additional 3 minutes or until no longer pink.
3. Stir in the tomato paste, broth, salt, pepper, paprika, and bay leaf. Cover and let it simmer over low-medium heat approximately 30 minutes.
4. Stir in Creme fraiche; turn off the heat and stir until everything is well combined. Ladle into serving bowls and serve immediately.

24. Cheesy and Buttery Pork Chops

If you are short on time, these pork chops with cheese, spices and butter are faster than ordering takeout. You can use any full-fat, firm cheese of your choice.

Servings 2

Ready in about

NUTRITIONAL INFORMATION (Per serving)

494 - Calories
39.8g - Fat
5.3g - Carbs
1.1g - Fiber
28.6g - Protein
2.7g - Sugars

Ingredients

- 1/2 stick butter, room temperature
- 1/2 cup white onion, chopped
- 4 ounces button mushrooms, sliced
- 1/3 pound pork loin chops
- 1 teaspoon dried parsley flakes
- Salt and ground black pepper, to taste
- 1/2 cup Swiss cheese, shredded

Directions

1. Melt 1/4 of the butter stick in a skillet over medium heat. Then, sauté the onions and mushrooms until the onions are translucent and the mushrooms are tender and fragrant, about 5 minutes. Reserve.
2. Then, melt the remaining 1/4 of the butter stick and cook pork until slightly browned on all sides, about 10 minutes.
3. Add the onion mixture, parsley, salt, and pepper. Lastly, top with cheese; cover and let it cook on medium-low heat until cheese has melted.
4. Serve immediately and enjoy!

25. Filipino Nilaga Soup

You can use a slow cooker to cook this soup; cook on high for 4 hours or until the meat is fork-tender. You can also add beef chuck roast or ribs and cook it all together.

Servings 4

Ready in about 45 minutes

NUTRITIONAL INFORMATION (Per Serving)

203 - Calories
8.4g - Fat
3.7g - Carbs
1.1g - Fiber
27.1g - Protein
1.7g - Sugars

Ingredients

- 1 teaspoon butter
- 1 pound pork ribs, boneless and cut into small pieces
- 1 shallot, chopped
- 2 garlic cloves, minced
- 1 (1/2-inch) piece fresh ginger, chopped
- 1 cup water
- 2 cups chicken stock
- 1 tablespoon patis (fish sauce)
- 1 cup fresh tomatoes, pureed
- 1 cup cauliflower "rice"
- Sea salt and ground black pepper, to taste

Directions

1. Melt the butter in a pot over medium-high heat. Then, cook the pork ribs on all sides for 5 to 6 minutes.
2. Add the shallot, garlic and ginger; cook an additional 3 minutes. Add the remaining ingredients.
3. Let it cook, covered, for 30 to 35 minutes. Ladle into individual bowls and serve.

26. Pork Tenderloin with Southern Cabbage

You can marinate pork for a foolproof tenderloin if desired. Professional cooks add a bit of lemon juice to the cabbage while cooking.

Servings 2

Ready in about 25 minutes

NUTRITIONAL INFORMATION (Per Serving)

254 - Calories
10.8g - Fat
5.7g - Carbs
1.6g - Fiber
31.8g - Protein
3.3g - Sugars

Ingredients

The Pork tenderloin:
- 1/2 pound pork tenderloin
- Celtic sea salt and freshly cracked black pepper, to taste
- 1/2 teaspoon granulated garlic
- 1/4 teaspoon ginger powder
- 1/2 teaspoon dried sage
- 1 tablespoon lard, room temperature

The Cabbage:
- 4 ounces cabbage, sliced into strips
- 1/3 cup vegetable broth
- 2 tablespoons sherry wine
- 1/2 teaspoon mustard seeds
- Celtic sea salt, to taste
- 1/2 teaspoon black peppercorns

Directions

1. Season the pork with salt, black pepper, granulated garlic, ginger powder, and sage.
2. Melt the lard in a pan over moderate heat. Sear the pork for 7 to 8 minutes, turning periodically.
3. In a pan that is preheated over medium heat, bring the cabbage, broth, sherry, and mustard seeds to a boil over high heat.
4. Season with salt and black peppercorns; cook, stirring periodically, until the cabbage is tender, about 12 minutes; do not overcook.
5. Serve the pork with sautéed cabbage on the side. Bon appétit!

27. Indian-Style Fried Pork

Pork shoulder is the perfect cut for this recipe; it has a great meat to fat ratio. Serve with mashed cauliflower and you will have a perfect ketogenic, family meal.

Servings 4

Ready in about 15 minutes

NUTRITIONAL INFORMATION (Per Serving)

478 - Calories
34.7g - Fat
2.2g - Carbs
0g - Fiber
36.4g - Protein
0.3g - Sugars

Ingredients

- 1 teaspoon shallot powder
- 1 teaspoon porcini powder
- 1 teaspoon garlic powder
- 1/2 teaspoon cumin
- 1/4 teaspoon turmeric powder
- 1 cinnamon stick
- 2 dried Kashmiri red chillies, roasted
- Sea salt and ground black pepper, to taste
- 1 pound pork shoulder
- 1/2 cup ground pork rinds
- 1/2 cup Parmesan cheese, grated
- 2 eggs
- 2 tablespoons tallow

Directions

1. Blend the spices together with the cinnamon and chillies until you have a smooth paste. Rub this paste all over the pork shoulder.
2. In a bowl, combine the pork rinds with parmesan cheese. In a separate bowl, whisk the eggs.
3. Slice the pork into small pieces; dip the pork in the egg and then, cover it with the pork rind mixture.
4. Melt the tallow in a skillet over medium-high heat. Cook the pork for 2 to 3 minutes per side. Bon appétit!

BEEF

28. Italian-Style Spicy Meatballs

Are you in the mood for meatballs? Enjoy all the satisfying flavors of Italian cuisine in these spicy and cheesy meatballs.

Servings 3

Ready in about 15 minutes

NUTRITIONAL INFORMATION (Per Serving)

458 Calories
35.8g Fat
4.3g Carbs
0.2g Fiber
28.2g Protein
3.1g Sugars

Ingredients

Sauce:
• 3 ounces Asiago cheese, grated
• 1/4 cup mayonnaise
• 1 chili pepper, minced
• 1 teaspoon yellow mustard
• 1 teaspoon Italian parsley
• 1/2 teaspoon red pepper flakes, crushed
• 1/2 teaspoon sea salt
• 1/2 teaspoon ground black pepper

Meatballs:
• 1/2 pound ground beef
• 1 egg
• 1 tablespoon olive oil

Directions

1. In a bowl, thoroughly combine the cheese, mayo, chili, mustard, parsley, red pepper, salt, and black pepper.
2. Then, stir in the ground beef and egg. Stir to combine well. Shape the mixture into meatballs.
3. Now, heat the oil in a skillet over a moderate flame. Once hot, cook the meatballs for 2 to 3 minutes on each side. Serve and enjoy!

29. Rich Double-Cheese Meatloaf

This is the perfect blend of deliciousness and comfort. It's a great idea for the next holiday.

Servings 4

Ready in about 1 hour

NUTRITIONAL INFORMATION (Per Serving)

361 - Calories
23.1g - Fat
5.6g - Carbs
0.8g - Fiber
32.2g - Protein
2.5g - Sugars

Ingredients

- 2 teaspoons sunflower oil
- 1/2 cup onions, chopped
- 2 cloves garlic, minced
- 1 bell pepper, seeded and chopped
- 1 jalapeno pepper, seeded and chopped
- 3/4 pound ground beef
- 1/4 pound bacon, chopped
- 1/2 Swiss cheese, grated
- 1/2 cup Parmesan cheese, grated
- 1 egg, whisked
- 1 teaspoon oyster sauce
- Sea salt and ground black pepper, to taste
- 1 ripe tomato, pureed
- 1 teaspoon Dijon mustard

Directions

1. Start by preheating your oven to 390 degrees F. Lightly grease a baking pan with a nonstick cooking spray.
2. Heat the oil in a pan over a moderate flame. Now, sauté the onions, garlic, and peppers until tender and aromatic, about 5 minutes.
3. In a mixing bowl, thoroughly combine the ground beef, bacon, cheese, egg, oyster sauce, salt, and ground black pepper. Form the mixture into a loaf and press it into the baking pan; spread the mixture of pureed tomato and mustard over the top.
4. Cover the dish with foil and bake for 50 minutes in the preheated oven. Enjoy!

30. Meat and Goat Cheese Stuffed Mushrooms

You can serve these mushrooms as the perfect complement to any keto dinner or a complete meal, it's up to you. In less than 25 minutes you can have a great dish that everyone loves.

Servings 5

Ready in about 25 minutes

NUTRITIONAL INFORMATION (Per Serving)

148 - Calories
8.4g - Fat
4.8g - Carbs
1.1g - Fiber
14.1g - Protein
2.7g - Sugars

Ingredients

- 4 ounces ground beef
- 2 ounces ground pork
- Kosher salt and ground black pepper, to taste
- 1/4 cup goat cheese, crumbled
- 2 tablespoons Romano cheese, grated
- 2 tablespoons shallot, minced
- 1 garlic clove, minced
- 1 teaspoon dried basil
- 1/2 teaspoon dried oregano
- 1/2 teaspoon dried rosemary
- 20 button mushrooms, stems removed

Direction

1. Combine all ingredients, except for the mushrooms, in a mixing bowl. Then, stuff the mushrooms with this filling.
2. Bake in the preheated oven at 370 degrees F approximately 18 minutes. Serve warm or cold. Bon appétit!

31. Shredded Beef with Herbs

Try something authentic and make this dish for the next family gathering!
Serve shredded beef over keto tacos or cauliflower rice.

Servings 4

**Ready in about
50 minutes**

**NUTRITIONAL
INFORMATION
(Per Serving)**

421 - Calories
35.7g - Fat
5.9g - Carbs
1g - Fiber
19.7g - Protein
2.7g - Sugars

Ingredients

- 1 tablespoon olive oil
- 1 pound rib eye, cut into strips
- 2 tablespoons rice wine
- 1/4 cup beef bone broth
- Sea salt and ground black pepper, to taste
- 2 tablespoons fresh parsley, finely chopped
- 2 tablespoons fresh chives, finely chopped
- 2 chipotle peppers in adobo sauce, chopped
- 1 garlic clove, crushed
- 2 small-sized ripe tomatoes, pureed
- 1 yellow onion, peeled and chopped
- 1/2 teaspoon dry mustard
- 1 teaspoon dried basil
- 1 teaspoon dried marjoram

Directions

1. Heat the oil in a pan over medium-high heat. Sear the beef for 6 to 7 minutes, stirring periodically. Work in batches.
2. Add the remaining ingredients, reduce the heat to medium-low and let it cook for 40 minutes.
3. Shred the beef and serve. Bon appétit!

32. Chinese Ground Beef Skillet

When you fancy a beef stir-fry with Asian flavors, try this recipe. The key ingredients to the best Chinese food include soy sauce, rice wine, and brown mushrooms.

Servings 3

Ready in about 15 minutes

NUTRITIONAL INFORMATION (Per Serving)

179 - Calories
10.4g - Fat
5.8g - Carbs
1g - Fiber
16.5g - Protein
2.6g - Sugars

Ingredients

- 1 tablespoon sesame oil
- 1/2 pound ground chuck
- 1 shallot, minced
- 1 garlic clove, minced
- 1 (1/2-inch) piece ginger root, peeled and grated
- 1 bell pepper, seeded and sliced
- 4 ounces brown mushrooms, sliced
- 1 teaspoon tamari soy sauce
- 1 tablespoon rice wine
- 2 whole star anise
- Himalayan salt and ground black pepper, to taste

Directions

1. Heat the oil in a pan over a moderate flame. Now, cook the ground chuck until it is no longer pink. Reserve.
2. Then, cook the shallot, garlic, ginger, pepper, and mushrooms in pan drippings. Add the remaining ingredients along with reserved beef to the pan.
3. Reduce the heat to medium-low; let it simmer for 2 to 3 minutes longer. Make sure to stir continuously. Enjoy!

33. Easy Steak Salad

Sometimes you just want a simple salad for lunch. You can make a satisfying keto salad from start to finish in under 20 minutes.

Servings 4

Ready in about

NUTRITIONAL INFORMATION (Per Serving)

231 - Calories
17.1g - Fat
6g - Carbs
3.4g - Fiber
13.8g - Protein
1.5g - Sugars

Ingredients

- 2 tablespoons olive oil
- 8 ounces flank steak, salt-and-pepper-seasoned
- 1 cucumber, sliced
- 1/2 cup onions, finely sliced
- 1 ripe avocado, peeled and sliced
- 2 medium-sized heirloom tomatoes, sliced
- 2 ounces baby arugula
- 1 tablespoon fresh coriander, chopped
- 3 tablespoons lime juice

Directions

1. Heat 1 tablespoon of olive oil in a pan over medium-high heat. Cook the flank steak for 5 minutes, turning once or twice.
2. Let stand for 10 minutes; then, slice thinly across the grain. Transfer the meat to a bowl.
3. Add cucumbers, shallots, avocado, tomatoes, baby arugula, and fresh coriander. Now, drizzle your salad with lime juice and the remaining 1 tablespoon of olive oil.
4. Serve well chilled and enjoy!

34. Saucy Skirt Steak with Broccoli

Broccoli is the perfect ingredient when we need a little something extra to round out our keto meal. Besides being delicious, broccoli has many health benefits.

Servings 3

Ready in about 15 minutes + marinating time

NUTRITIONAL INFORMATION (Per Serving)

331 - Calories
24.7g - Fat
4.5g - Carbs
2.8g - Fiber
24.1g - Protein
0.9g - Sugars

Ingredients

- 1/2 pound skirt steak, sliced into pieces
- 2 tablespoons butter, room temperature
- 1/2 pound broccoli, cut into florets
- 1/2 cup scallions, chopped
- 1 clove garlic, pressed

Marinade:
- 1/2 teaspoon ground black pepper
- 1 teaspoon red pepper flakes
- 1/2 teaspoon sea salt
- 2 tablespoons olive oil
- 1 tablespoon tamari sauce
- 1/4 cup wine vinegar

Directions

1. In a ceramic bowl, thoroughly combine all ingredients for the marinade. Add the beef and allow it to sit in your refrigerator for 2 hours.
2. Melt 1 tablespoon of butter in a skillet over high to medium-high heat. Cook the broccoli for 2 minutes, stirring frequently, until it is tender but bright green. Reserve.
3. Melt the remaining tablespoon of butter in the skillet. Once hot, cook the scallions and garlic until aromatic, about 2 minutes. Reserve.
4. Next, sear the beef, adding a small amount of the marinade. Cook until well browned on all sides or about 10 minutes.
5. Add the reserved vegetables and cook for a few minutes more or until everything is heated through. Bon appétit!

35. Classic Beef Stroganoff

Beef stew meat is easier to slice if it's partially frozen. Sautéing the garlic and onion will help define their unique taste but you can skip this step if you are in a hurry.

Servings 4

Ready in about 1 hour

NUTRITIONAL INFORMATION (Per Serving)

303 - Calories
17.2g - Fat
5.6g - Carbs
0.9g - Fiber
32.4g - Protein
1.8g - Sugars

Ingredients

- 2 tablespoons lard, room temperature
- 1 pound beef stew meat, cut across grain into strips
- 1/2 yellow onion, peeled and chopped
- 2 garlic cloves, minced
- 4 ounces fresh mushrooms, sliced
- 1/2 teaspoon salt
- 1 teaspoon smoked paprika
- 1/4 teaspoon black pepper
- 1/2 teaspoon dried basil
- 1/4 cup red cooking wine
- 4 cups vegetable broth
- 1 fresh tomato, pureed
- 2 celery stalks, chopped
- 1/2 cup sour cream

Directions

1. Melt the lard in a stockpot over medium heat. Then, cook the meat until nicely browned on all sides.
2. Then, add onion and garlic and cook until they are fragrant. Now, stir in the mushrooms and cook until they are tender.
3. Add seasonings, wine, broth, tomato, and celery. Reduce heat, cover, and simmer for 50 minutes.
4. Turn off the heat and add sour cream; stir until heated through. Taste, adjust the seasonings, and serve warm. Bon appétit!

FISH & SEAFOOD

36. Catfish and Cauliflower Casserole

Fresh aromatics and dried herbs give this seafood casserole an extra special taste. Your family will definitely ask for more!

Servings 4

Ready in about 30 minutes

NUTRITIONAL INFORMATION (Per Serving)

510 - Calories
40g - Fat
5.5g - Carbs
1.6g - Fiber
31.3g - Protein
3g - Sugars

Ingredients

- 1 tablespoon sesame oil
- 11 ounces cauliflower
- 4 scallions
- 1 garlic clove, minced
- 1 teaspoon fresh ginger root, grated
- Salt and ground black pepper, to taste
- Cayenne pepper, to taste
- 2 sprigs dried thyme, crushed
- 1 sprig rosemary, crushed
- 24 ounces catfish, cut into pieces
- 1/2 cup cream cheese
- 1/2 cup double cream
- 1 egg
- 2 ounces butter, cold

Directions

1. Start by preheating your oven to 390 degrees F. Now, lightly grease a casserole dish with a nonstick cooking spray.
2. Then, heat the oil in a pan over medium-high heat; once hot, cook the cauliflower and scallions until tender or 5 to 6 minutes. Add the garlic and ginger; continue to sauté 1 minute more.
3. Transfer the vegetables to the prepared casserole dish. Sprinkle with seasonings. Add catfish to the top.
4. In a mixing bowl, thoroughly combine the cream cheese, double cream, and egg. Spread this creamy mixture over the top of your casserole.
5. Top with slices of butter. Bake in the preheated oven for 18 to 22 minutes or until the fish flakes easily with a fork. Bon appétit!

37. Swedish Herring Salad

I created this salad after falling in love with Surströmming (Swedish for a lightly salted fermented Baltic Sea herring). This makes a perfect holiday salad as well.

Servings 3

Ready in about 10 minutes

NUTRITIONAL INFORMATION (Per Serving)

134 - Calories
7.9g - Fat
5.4g - Carbs
1g - Fiber
10.2g - Protein
2.3g - Sugars

Ingredients

- 6 ounces pickled herring pieces, drained and flaked
- 1/2 cup baby spinach
- 2 tablespoons fresh basil leaves
- 2 tablespoons fresh chives, chopped
- 1 teaspoon garlic, minced
- 1 bell pepper, chopped
- 1 red onion, chopped
- 2 tablespoons key lime juice, freshly squeezed
- Sea salt and ground black pepper, to taste

Directions

1. In a salad bowl, combine the herring pieces with spinach, basil leaves, chives, garlic, bell pepper, and red onion.
2. Then, drizzle key lime juice over the salad; add salt and pepper to taste and toss to combine. Smaklig måltid! Bon appétit!

38. Hearty Fisherman's Stew

Try an all-star recipe for a fish stew with a Mediterranean twist! You can use frozen or fresh ingredients; anyway, it will taste good.

Servings 4

Ready in about 30 minutes

NUTRITIONAL INFORMATION (Per Serving)

271 - Calories
19.5g - Fat
4.8g - Carbs
1g - Fiber
18.5g - Protein
1.3g - Sugars

Ingredients

- 1 tablespoon tallow, room temperature
- 1 red onion, chopped
- 2 garlic cloves, smashed
- 1 jalapeno pepper, chopped
- 1/2 bunch fresh dill, roughly chopped
- 1 ripe fresh tomato, pureed
- 1 cup shellfish stock
- 2 cups water
- 1 pound halibut, cut into bite-sized chunks
- Sea salt and ground black pepper, to taste
- 1 teaspoon cayenne pepper
- 1/2 teaspoon curry powder
- 2 bay leaves

Directions

1. Melt the tallow in a large pot over medium-high heat. Then, sweat the onion for 3 minutes; stir in the garlic and jalapeno pepper and sauté a minute more.
2. Add fresh dill and tomato; cook for 8 minutes more. Pour in shellfish stock and water. Add salt, black pepper, cayenne pepper, curry powder, and bay leaves.
3. Reduce to a simmer; cook until everything is thoroughly cooked or for 15 minutes. Taste and adjust the seasonings. Ladle into soup bowls and serve warm. Enjoy!

39. Fish and Vegetable Medley

Cod may replace the snapper, and other keto veggies may be used, such as green beans or bell peppers. Snapper is a lean source of protein that is loaded with vitamin A, potassium, omega-3 fatty acids, and essential minerals.

Servings 4

Ready in about 20 minutes

NUTRITIONAL INFORMATION (Per Serving)

151 - Calories
3g - Fat
5.8g - Carbs
1.5g - Fiber
24.4g - Protein
2.8g - Sugars

Ingredients

- 1 teaspoon sesame oil
- 1/2 cup scallions, thinly sliced
- 1/2 teaspoon fresh ginger, grated
- 1/2 teaspoon garlic, crushed
- 1 teaspoon red curry paste
- 2 whole star anise
- 1 teaspoon smoked paprika
- 2 ripe tomatoes, crushed
- Coarse sea salt and ground black pepper, to taste
- 1 pound snapper, cut into bite-sized pieces

Directions

1. Heat the oil in a pot over moderate heat. Cook the scallion until tender and aromatic; now, add ginger and garlic and cook an additional 40 seconds, stirring frequently.
2. Add the remaining ingredients and reduce the heat to medium-low. Let it simmer for 15 minutes or until the fish flakes easily with a fork. Bon appétit!

40. Salmon Curry with a Twist

As for seasonings, some people do not prefer strong spices, as they like to keep the salmon flavor dominant. You can also add garam masala and ginger-garlic paste to this curry.

Servings 4

Ready in about

NUTRITIONAL INFORMATION (Per Serving)

246 - Calories
16.2g - Fat
4.9g - Carbs
0.6g - Fiber
20.3g - Protein
2.1g - Sugars

Ingredients

- 1 tablespoon coconut oil
- 1/2 cup leeks, chopped
- 1 teaspoon garlic, smashed
- 1 Thai chili pepper, seeded and minced
- 1 teaspoon turmeric powder
- 1/2 teaspoon cumin
- 4 ounces double cream
- 2 ounces full-fat coconut milk, canned
- 1 cup fish stock
- 1 cup water
- 3/4 pound salmon, cut into bite-sized chunks
- Salt and ground black pepper, to taste
- 1/4 cup fresh cilantro, roughly chopped

Directions

1. Heat the oil in a stockpot over medium-high heat. Now, sauté the leeks and garlic for 2 to 3 minutes, stirring frequently.
2. Add chili pepper, turmeric, and cumin; cook an additional minute. Add cream, coconut milk, fish stock, water, salmon, salt, and black pepper.
3. Reduce the heat and let it simmer approximately 12 minutes.
4. Afterwards, ladle into individual bowls; serve topped with fresh cilantro leaves and enjoy!

41. Tuna, Avocado and Ham Wraps

Ahi tuna aka yellowfin tuna is one of the favorite keto foods since it is a diet-friendly and full of protein. It is loaded with selenium, phosphorus, potassium, vitamin D, and vitamin B-12.

Servings 3

Ready in about 10 minutes + chilling time

NUTRITIONAL INFORMATION (Per Serving)

308 - Calories
19.9g - Fat
4.3g - Carbs
2.5g - Fiber
27.8g - Protein
0.8g - Sugars

Ingredients

- 1/2 cup dry white wine
- 1/2 cup water
- 1/2 teaspoon mixed peppercorns
- 1/2 teaspoon dry mustard powder
- 1/2 pound ahi tuna steak
- 6 slices of ham
- 1/2 Hass avocado, peeled, pitted and sliced
- 1 tablespoon fresh lemon juice
- 6 lettuce leaves

Directions

1. Add wine, water, peppercorns, and mustard powder to a skillet and bring to a boil. Add the tuna and simmer gently for 3 minutes to 5 minutes per side.
2. Discard the cooking liquid and slice tuna into bite-sized pieces. Divide the tuna pieces between slices of ham.
3. Add avocado and drizzle with fresh lemon. Roll the wraps up and place each wrap on a lettuce leaf. Serve well chilled. Bon appétit!

42. Alaskan Cod with Mustard Cream Sauce

Alaskan cod fillets with mustard cream sauce is an easy recipe that delivers the best flavors from common ingredients. It's perfect for any type of ketogenic diet.

Servings 4

Ready in about 10 minutes

NUTRITIONAL INFORMATION (Per Serving)

166 - Calories
8.2g - Fat
2.6g - Carbs
0.3g - Fiber
19.8g - Protein
1.9g - Sugars

Ingredients

- 1 tablespoon coconut oil
- 4 Alaskan cod fillets
- Salt and freshly ground black pepper, to taste
- 6 leaves basil, chiffonade
- Mustard Cream Sauce:
- 1 teaspoon yellow mustard
- 1 teaspoon paprika
- 1/4 teaspoon ground bay leaf
- 3 tablespoons cream cheese
- 1/2 cup Greek-style yogurt
- 1 garlic clove, minced
- 1 teaspoon lemon zest
- 1 tablespoon fresh parsley, minced
- Sea salt and ground black pepper, to taste

Directions

1. Heat coconut oil in a pan over medium heat. Sear the fish for 2 to 3 minutes per side. Season with salt and ground black pepper.
2. Mix all ingredients for the sauce until everything is well combined. Top the fish fillets with the sauce and serve garnished with fresh basil leaves. Bon appétit!

43. Smoked Haddock Fish Burgers

The scallions and Parmesan in this easy haddock burger recipe pair wonderfully with chili powder. Serve on keto burger buns, if desired.

Servings 4

Ready in about 20 minutes

NUTRITIONAL INFORMATION (Per Serving)

174 - Calories
11.4g - Fat
1.5g - Carbs
0.2g - Fiber
15.4g - Protein
0.3g - Sugars

Ingredients

- 2 tablespoons sunflower oil
- 8 ounces smoked haddock
- 1 egg
- 1/4 cup Parmesan cheese, grated
- 1 teaspoon chili powder
- 1 teaspoon dried parsley flakes
- 1/4 cup scallions, chopped
- 1 teaspoon fresh garlic, minced
- Salt and ground black pepper, to taste
- 4 lemon wedges

Directions

1. Heat 1 tablespoon of oil in a pan over medium-high heat. Cook the haddock for 6 minutes or until just cooked through; discard the skin and bones and flake into small pieces.
2. Mix the smoked haddock, egg, cheese, chili powder, parsley, scallions, garlic, salt, and black pepper in a large bowl.
3. Heat the remaining tablespoon of oil and cook fish burgers until they are well cooked in the middle or about 6 minutes. Garnish each serving with a lemon wedge.

EGGS & DAIRY

44. Paprika Omelet with Goat Cheese

You can make this go-to omelet every morning to wake up your metabolism. You can use different fillings such as bacon, ham, peppers, or spinach. In addition, breakfast is ready in less than 10 minutes.

Servings 2

Ready in about 10 minutes

NUTRITIONAL INFORMATION (Per Serving)

287 - Calories
22.6g - Fat
1.3g - Carbs
0g - Fiber
19.8g - Protein
1.3g - Sugars

Ingredients

- 2 teaspoons ghee, room temperature
- 4 eggs, whisked
- 4 tablespoons goat cheese
- 1 teaspoon paprika
- Sea salt and ground black pepper, to taste

Directions

1. Melt the ghee in a pan over medium heat.
2. Add the whisked eggs to the pan and cover with the lid; reduce the heat to medium-low.
3. Cook for 4 minutes; now, stir in the cheese and paprika; continue to cook an additional 3 minutes or until cheese has melted.
4. Season with salt and pepper and serve immediately. Enjoy!

45. Dilly Boiled Eggs with Avocado

Nothing beats a classic! The only thing better than boiled eggs is perfectly boiled eggs served with fresh avocado slices.

Servings 3

Ready in about 10 minutes

NUTRITIONAL INFORMATION (Per Serving)

222 - Calories
17.6g - Fat
5.7g - Carbs
3.9g - Fiber
12.2g - Protein
0.9g - Sugars

Ingredients

- 6 eggs
- 1/2 teaspoon kosher salt
- 1/2 teaspoon ground black pepper
- 1/2 teaspoon cayenne pepper
- 1/2 teaspoon dried dill weed
- 1 avocado, pitted and sliced
- 1 tablespoon lemon juice

Directions

1. Place the eggs in a pan of boiling water; then, cook over low heat for 6 minutes.
2. Peel and halve the eggs. Sprinkle the eggs with salt, black pepper, cayenne pepper, and dill.
3. Serve on individual plates; drizzle the avocado slices with fresh lemon juice and serve with eggs. Enjoy!

46. Greek-Style Frittata with Herbs

Mediterranean ingredients make this frittata a breakfast staple during the summer months. However, you can serve this impressive dish on any occasion.

Servings 4

Ready in about 30 minutes

NUTRITIONAL INFORMATION (Per Serving)

345 - Calories
28.5g - Fat
4.4g - Carbs
0.6g - Fiber
18.2g - Protein
2.3g - Sugars

Ingredients

- 6 eggs
- 1/2 cup heavy cream
- 2 tablespoons Greek-style yogurt
- 2 ounces bacon, chopped
- Sea salt and freshly ground black pepper, to taste
- 1 tablespoon olive oil
- 1/2 cup red onions, peeled and sliced
- 1 garlic clove, finely chopped
- 8 Kalamata olives, pitted and sliced
- 1 teaspoon dried oregano
- 1/2 teaspoon dried rosemary
- 1/2 teaspoon dried marjoram
- 4 ounces Feta cheese, crumbled

Directions

1. Preheat your oven to 360 degrees F. Sprits a baking pan with a nonstick cooking spray.
2. Mix the eggs, cream, yogurt, bacon, salt, and black pepper.
3. Heat the oil in a skillet over medium-high heat. Now, cook the onion and garlic until tender and fragrant, about 3 minutes. Transfer the mixture to the prepared baking pan.
4. Pour the egg mixture over the vegetables. Add olives, oregano, rosemary, and marjoram.
5. Bake approximately 13 minutes, until the eggs are set. Scatter feta cheese over the top and bake an additional 3 minutes. Let it sit for 5 minutes; slice into wedges and serve.

47. Mangalorean Egg Curry

—◦◦◦—

Eggs in a spicy coconut gravy! Make this delicious melange of eggs, tomatoes, and southern spices for lunch or dinner.

Servings 4

Ready in about

NUTRITIONAL INFORMATION (Per Serving)

305 - Calories
16.4g - Fat
5.7g - Carbs
1.1g - Fiber
32.2g - Protein
4.3g - Sugars

Ingredients

- 2 tablespoons rice bran oil
- 1/2 cup scallions, chopped
- 1 teaspoon Kashmiri chili powder
- 1/4 teaspoon carom seeds
- 1/4 teaspoon methi seeds
- Kosher salt and ground black pepper, to taste
- 2 ripe tomatoes, pureed
- 2 teaspoons tamarind paste
- 1/2 cup chicken stock
- 4 boiled egg, peeled
- 1 teaspoon curry paste
- 2 tablespoons curry leaves
- 1/2 teaspoon cinnamon powder
- 1/2 cup coconut milk
- 1 tablespoon cilantro leaves

Directions

1. Heat the oil in a pan over medium heat. Now, cook the scallions and chili until tender and fragrant.
2. Add carom seeds, methi seeds, salt, pepper, and tomatoes; cook for a further 8 minutes.
3. Then, add the tamarind paste and chicken stock. Reduce the heat to medium-low and cook for 3 minutes more.
4. Add the eggs, curry paste, curry leaves, cinnamon powder, and coconut milk. Let it simmer for 6 minutes more. Garnish with cilantro leaves. Bon appétit!

48. Egg, Bacon and Kale Muffins

These muffins are ooey-gooey mini frittatas and they are kid-friendly too.
They couldn't be easier to make!

Servings 4

**Ready in about
25 minutes**

**NUTRITIONAL
INFORMATION
(Per Serving)**

384 - Calories
29.8g - Fat
5.1g - Carbs
1.1g - Fiber
24g - Protein
2.4g - Sugars

Ingredients

- 1/2 cup bacon
- 1 shallot, chopped
- 1 garlic clove, minced
- 1 cup kale
- 1 ripe tomato, chopped
- 6 eggs
- 1 cup Asiago cheese, shredded
- Salt and black pepper, to taste
- 1 teaspoon dried rosemary
- 1/2 teaspoon dried basil
- 1/2 teaspoon dried marjoram

Directions

1. Start by preheating your oven to 390 degrees F. Add muffin liners to a muffin tin.
2. Preheat your pan over medium heat. Cook the bacon for 3 to 4 minutes; now, chop the bacon and reserve.
3. Now, cook the shallots and garlic in the bacon fat until they are tender. Add the remaining ingredients and mix to combine well.
4. Pour the batter into muffin cups and bake for 13 minutes or until the edges are slightly browned.
5. Allow your muffins to stand for 5 minutes before removing from the tin. Bon appétit!

49. Cheesy Brussels Sprouts

Brussels sprouts are loaded with vitamin K, fiber, and antioxidants. Sesame oil is helpful in lowering blood sugar levels.

Servings 4

Ready in about 25 minutes

NUTRITIONAL INFORMATION (Per Serving)

202 - Calories
16.3g - Fat
5.8g - Carbs
2.3g - Fiber
8.8g - Protein
1.9g - Sugars

Ingredients

- 3/4 pound Brussels sprouts, cleaned and halved
- 2 tablespoons sesame oil
- 1 teaspoon dried parsley flakes
- 1 sprig dried thyme
- Kosher salt and ground black pepper, to taste
- 6 ounces Colby cheese, shredded

Directions

1. Start by preheating your oven to 400 degrees F.
2. Lightly grease a baking pan with a nonstick cooking spray. Arrange the Brussels sprouts on the baking pan. Drizzle them with peanut oil.
3. Toss with parsley, thyme, salt, and black pepper. Roast in the preheated oven approximately 18 minutes.
4. Add Colby cheese and roast an additional 3 minutes. Serve immediately. Enjoy!

50. Cauliflower, Cheese and Egg Fat Bombs

These fat bombs aren't just delicious, they're inexpensive, diet-friendly, and kid-friendly! They deserve a spot on your holiday table!

Servings 4

Ready in about 35 minutes

NUTRITIONAL INFORMATION (Per Serving)

168 - Calories
10.9g - Fat
3.5g - Carbs
1.1g - Fiber
13.9g - Protein
1.4g - Sugars

Ingredients

- 1/2 pound cauliflower, cut into florets
- 1/2 cup pork rinds, crushed
- 1/4 cup almond flour
- 1/2 cup Romano cheese, grated
- 2 eggs, beaten

Directions

1. Boil the cauliflower until tender; drain well. Then, mix the cauliflower with pork rinds, almond flour, Romano cheese, and eggs; shape the mixture into bite-sized balls.
2. Arrange the balls in a parchment-lined baking pan.
3. Bake in the preheated oven at 345 degrees F approximately 28 minutes. Serve warm or cold and enjoy!

51. Double Cheese and Sausage Balls

It's easy to make a delicious keto appetizer in less than 20 minutes. If you love breakfast sausage and cheese, this is the perfect bite for you!

Servings 3

Ready in about

NUTRITIONAL INFORMATION
(Per Serving)

412 - Calories
34.6g - Fat
4.7g - Carbs
0.1g - Fiber
19.6g - Protein
1.7g - Sugars

Ingredients

- 1/2 pound breakfast sausage
- 1/2 cup almond flour
- 1/2 cup Colby cheese, shredded
- 4 tablespoons Romano cheese, freshly grated
- 1 egg
- 1 garlic clove, pressed
- 2 tablespoons fresh chives, minced

Directions

1. Thoroughly combine all ingredients in a mixing bowl; mix until everything is well incorporated.
2. Shape the mixture into balls and arrange them on a parchment-lined cookie sheet. Bake in the preheated oven at 360 degrees F for about 18 minutes.
3. Serve warm or cold. Bon appétit!

VEGETARIAN

52. Mexican Inspired Stuffed Peppers

These vegetarian stuffed peppers are filled with cheese, eggs, and spices, then, cooked in the tomato-mustard sauce. You can par-boiling bell peppers in a salted, boiling water in the beginning.

Servings 3

Ready in about 45 minutes

NUTRITIONAL INFORMATION (Per Serving)

194 - Calories
13.9g - Fat
3.5g - Carbs
0.7g - Fiber
13.3g - Protein
2.4g - Sugars

Ingredients

- 3 bell peppers, halved, seeds removed
- 3 eggs, whisked
- 1 cup Mexican cheese blend
- 1 teaspoon chili powder
- 1 garlic clove, minced
- 1 teaspoon onion powder
- 1 ripe tomato, pureed
- 1 teaspoon mustard powder

Directions

1. Start by preheating your oven to 370 degrees F. Spritz the bottom and sides of a baking pan with a cooking oil.
2. In a mixing bowl, thoroughly combine the eggs, cheese, chili powder, garlic, and onion powder. Divide the filling between the bell peppers.
3. Mix the tomatoes with mustard powder and transfer the mixture to the baking pan. Cover with foil and bake for 40 minutes, until the peppers are tender and the filling is thoroughly heated. Bon appétit!

53. Frittata with Asparagus and Halloumi

Halloumi is a semi-hard cheese made from a mixture of goat's and sheep's milk that is widely used in Greek cuisine. Its deeply savoury flavour goes with eggs and asparagus very well.

Servings 4

Ready in about 25 minutes

NUTRITIONAL INFORMATION (Per Serving)

376 - Calories
29.1g - Fat
4g - Carbs
1g - Fiber
24.5g - Protein
2.5g - Sugars

Ingredients

- 1 tablespoon olive oil
- 1/2 red onion, sliced
- 4 ounces asparagus, cut into small chunks
- 1 tomato, chopped
- 5 whole eggs, beaten
- 10 ounces Halloumi cheese, crumbled
- 2 tablespoons green olives, pitted and sliced
- 1 tablespoon fresh parsley, chopped

Directions

1. Heat the oil in a skillet over medium-high heat; then, cook the onion and asparagus about 3 minutes, stirring continuously.
2. Next, add the tomato and cook for 2 minutes longer. Transfer the sautéed vegetables to a baking pan that is lightly greased with cooking oil.
3. Mix the eggs with cheese until well combined. Pour the mixture over the vegetables. Scatter sliced olives over the top. Bake in the preheated oven at 350 degrees F for 15 minutes.
4. Garnish with fresh parsley and serve immediately. Enjoy!

54. Baked Eggs and Cheese in Avocado

Here are picnic-worthy vegetarian bites! Asiago cheese adds a great firmness to these avocado shells like a glue that holds everything together.

Servings 4

Ready in about

NUTRITIONAL INFORMATION (Per Serving)

300 - Calories
24.6g - Fat
5.4g - Carbs
4.6g - Fiber
14.9g - Protein
0.5g - Sugars

Ingredients

- 2 avocados, pitted and halved
- 4 eggs
- Sea salt and freshly ground black pepper, to taste
- 1 cup Asiago cheese, grated
- 1/2 teaspoon red pepper flakes
- 1/2 teaspoon dried rosemary
- 1 tablespoon fresh chives, chopped

Directions

1. Crack the eggs into the avocado halves, keeping the yolks intact. Sprinkle with salt and black pepper.
2. Top with cheese, red pepper flakes, and rosemary. Arrange the stuffed avocado halves in a baking pan.
3. Bake in the preheated oven at 420 degrees F for about 15 minutes. Serve garnished with fresh chives. Enjoy!

55. Two-Cheese Zucchini Gratin

If you find your gratin watery after the 40 minutes, turn the temperature to 350 degrees F and bake for 10 minutes longer. Let it sit at least 20 minutes before slicing and serving.

Servings 5

Ready in about 50 minutes

NUTRITIONAL INFORMATION (Per Serving)

371 - Calories
32g - Fat
5.2g - Carbs
0.3g - Fiber
15.7g - Protein
2.6g - Sugars

Ingredients

- 10 large eggs
- 3 tablespoons yogurt
- 2 zucchini, sliced
- 1/2 medium-sized leek, sliced
- Sea salt and ground black pepper, to taste
- 1 teaspoon cayenne pepper
- 1 cup cream cheese
- 2 garlic cloves, minced
- 1 cup Swiss cheese, shredded

Directions

1. Start by preheating your oven to 360 degrees F. Then, spritz the bottom and sides of an oven proof pan with a nonstick cooking spray.
2. Then, mix the eggs with yogurt until well combined.
3. Overlap 1/2 of the zucchini and leek slices in the pan. Season with salt, black pepper, and cayenne pepper. Add cream cheese and minced garlic.
4. Add the remaining zucchini slices and leek. Add the egg mixture. Top with Swiss cheese. Bake for 40 minutes, until the top is golden brown. Bon appétit!

56. Italian Zuppa di Pomodoro

This Italian-inspired soup is loaded with antioxidant and nutrient dense vegetables as well as varous aromatics.

Servings 3

Ready in about 30 minutes

NUTRITIONAL INFORMATION (Per Serving)

137 - Calories
10.7g - Fat
5.6g - Carbs
1.2g - Fiber
5.6g - Protein
2.4g - Sugars

Ingredients

- 4 ounces broccoli
- 2 tablespoons sesame oil
- 1 small-sized onion, chopped
- 2 garlic cloves, minced
- 1 teaspoon cayenne pepper
- Sea salt and ground black pepper, to taste
- 1 cup spinach leaves, torn into pieces
- 1 celery stalk, peeled and chopped
- 2 cups vegetable broth
- 1 cup water
- 1 tomato, pureed
- 1 jalapeno pepper, minced
- 1 tablespoon Italian seasonings

Directions

1. Pulse the broccoli in your food processor until rice-sized pieces are formed; work in batches; reserve.
2. Then, heat the oil in a saucepan over medium heat. Then, sauté the onion and garlic until tender and aromatic.
3. Add the broccoli and cook for 2 minutes more. Add the remaining ingredients, except the spinach.
4. Bring to a rapid boil and then, immediately reduce the heat to medium-low. Now, simmer the soup approximately 25 minutes.
5. Add spinach, turn off the heat, and cover with the lid; let it wilt. Bon appétit!

57. Two-Cheese and Kale Bake

This vegetarian bake is overflowing with cheese and kale; it's so comforting and appetizing. You can use your favorite kind of cheese. Enjoy!

Servings 4

Ready in about 35 minutes

NUTRITIONAL INFORMATION (Per Serving)

384 - Calories
29.1g - Fat
5.9g - Carbs
1.5g - Fiber
25.1g - Protein
1.8g - Sugars

Ingredients

- Nonstick cooking spray
- 6 ounces kale, torn into pieces
- 4 eggs, whisked
- 1 cup Cheddar cheese, grated
- 1 cup Romano cheese
- 2 tablespoons sour cream
- 1 garlic clove, minced
- Sea salt, to taste
- 1/2 teaspoon ground black pepper, or more to taste
- 1/2 teaspoon cayenne pepper

Directions

1. Start by preheating your oven to 365 degrees F. Spritz the sides and bottom of a baking pan with a nonstick cooking spray.
2. Mix all ingredients and pour the mixture into the baking pan.
3. Bake for 30 to 35 minutes or until it is thoroughly heated. Bon appétit!

58. Grandma's Zucchini and Spinach Chowder

Keto recipes don't come much easier than this old-fashioned, vegetarian chowder. You can customize it with your favorite spices and keto mix-ins.

Servings 4

Ready in about 25 minutes

NUTRITIONAL INFORMATION (Per Serving)

85 - Calories
5.9g - Fat
3.8g - Carbs
1.3g - Fiber
3.7g - Protein
1.2g - Sugars

Ingredients

- 1 tablespoon olive oil
- 1 clove garlic, chopped
- 1/2 cup scallions, chopped
- 4 cups water
- 2 zucchini, sliced
- 1 celery stalk, chopped
- 2 tablespoons vegetable bouillon powder
- 4 ounces baby spinach
- Salt and ground black pepper, to taste
- 1 heaping tablespoon fresh parsley, chopped
- 1 tablespoon butter
- 1 egg, beaten

Directions

1. In a stockpot, heat the oil over medium-high heat. Now, cook the garlic and scallions until tender or about 4 minutes.
2. Add water, zucchini, celery, vegetable bouillon powder; cook for 13 minutes. Add spinach, salt, black pepper, parsley, and butter; cook for a further 5 minutes.
3. Then, stir in the egg and mix until well incorporated. Ladle into individual bowls and serve warm. Enjoy!

59. Crêpes with Peanut Butter and Coconut

If you can make scrambled eggs, then you can make these ketogenic crepes. Sure, it takes a little practice, but once you get the hang of it, you will be able to make the best crepes you have ever had.

Servings 5

Ready in about 50 minutes

NUTRITIONAL INFORMATION (Per Serving)

248 - Calories
21.7g - Fat
5.7g - Carbs
0.6g - Fiber
9.1g - Protein
1.9g - Sugars

Ingredients

- 4 eggs, well whisked
- 4 ounces cream cheese
- A pinch of salt
- 2 tablespoons coconut oil
- 3 tablespoons peanut butter
- 2 tablespoons toasted coconut

Directions

1. Whisk the eggs, cream cheese, and salt in a mixing bowl.
2. Heat the oil in a pancake frying pan over medium-high heat.
3. Fry each pancake for 4 to 5 minutes. Serve topped with peanut butter and coconut. Enjoy!

SNACKS & APPETIZERS

60. Lettuce Wraps with Ham and Cheese

You can use iceberg lettuce or even spinach and chard in this recipe.
Prepare this simple recipe ahead of time and enjoy your party to the fullest.

Servings 5

Ready in about 10 minutes

NUTRITIONAL INFORMATION (Per Serving)

148 - Calories
10.2g - Fat
4.2g - Carbs
0.8g - Fiber
10.7g - Protein
2.5g - Sugars

Ingredients

- 10 Boston lettuce leaves, washed and rinsed well
- 1 tablespoon lemon juice, freshly squeezed
- 10 tablespoons cream cheese
- 10 thin ham slices
- 1 tomato, chopped
- 1 red chili pepper, chopped

Directions

1. Drizzle lemon juice over the lettuce leaves. Spread cream cheese over the lettuce leaves. Add a ham slice on each leaf.
2. Divide chopped tomatoes between the lettuce leaves. Top with chili peppers and arrange on a nice serving platter. Bon appétit!

61. Ranch and Blue Cheese Dip

This tangy dipping sauce goes perfectly with chicken wings or vegetable sticks. Get your appetizer right with this quick and easy recipe!

Servings 10

Ready in about 10 minutes

NUTRITIONAL INFORMATION (Per Serving)

94 - Calories
8.1g - Fat
1.3g - Carbs
0.1g - Fiber
4.1g - Protein
0.7g - Sugars

Ingredients

- 1/2 cup Greek-style yogurt
- 1 cup blue cheese, crumbled
- 1/2 cup mayonnaise
- 1 tablespoon lime juice
- Freshly ground black pepper, to taste
- 2 tablespoons ranch seasoning

Directions

1. In a mixing bowl, thoroughly combine all ingredients until well incorporated.
2. Serve well chilled with your favorite keto dippers. Bon appétit!

62. Ranch Chicken Wings

The best part, these wings are easy to make and customizable to your personal taste preferences. Your guests will be coming back for more.

Servings 6

Ready in about 55 minutes

NUTRITIONAL INFORMATION (Per Serving)

466 - Calories
37.2g - Fat
1.9g - Carbs
0.1g - Fiber
28.6g - Protein
0.7g - Sugars

Ingredients

- 2 pounds chicken wings, pat dry
- Nonstick cooking spray
- Sea salt and cayenne pepper, to taste
- Ranch Dressing:
- 1/4 cup sour cream
- 1/4 cup buttermilk
- 1/2 cup mayonnaise
- 1/2 teaspoon lemon juice
- 1 tablespoon fresh parsley, minced
- 1 clove garlic, minced
- 2 tablespoons onion, finely chopped
- 1/4 teaspoon dry mustard
- Sea salt and ground black pepper, to taste

Directions

1. Start by preheating your oven to 420 degrees F.
2. Spritz the chicken wings with a cooking spray. Sprinkle the chicken wings with salt and cayenne pepper. Arrange the chicken wings on a parchment-lined baking pan.
3. Bake in the preheated oven for 50 minutes or until the wings are golden and crispy.
4. In the meantime, make the dressing by mixing all of the above ingredients. Serve with warm wings.

63. Colby Cheese-Stuffed Meatballs

Mozzarella cubes tucked inside meatballs! Serve these meatballs on a bed of fresh zucchini noodles (zoodles). Yummy!

Servings 8

Ready in about 25 minutes

NUTRITIONAL INFORMATION (Per Serving)

389 - Calories
31.3g - Fat
1.6g - Carbs
0.5g - Fiber
23.8g - Protein
0.8g - Sugars

Ingredients

- 1/2 pound ground pork
- 1 pound ground turkey
- 1 garlic clove, minced
- 4 tablespoons pork rinds, crushed
- 2 tablespoons shallots, chopped
- 4 ounces mozzarella string cheese, cubed
- 1 ripe tomato, pureed
- Salt and ground black pepper, to taste

Directions

1. In a mixing bowl, thoroughly combine all ingredients, except for the cheese. Shape the mixture into bite-sized balls.
2. Press 1 cheese cube into the center of each ball.
3. Place the meatballs on a parchment-lined baking sheet. Bake in the preheated oven at 350 degrees F for 18 to 25 minutes. Bon appétit!

64. Cheese and Artichoke Dip

This popular dip comes together in less than 25 minutes. And who can ever say no to this creamy goodness?

Servings 10

Ready in about 25 minutes

NUTRITIONAL INFORMATION
(Per Serving)

367 - Calories
31.7g - Fat
5.1g - Carbs
2.4g - Fiber
16.2g - Protein
1.7g - Sugars

Ingredients

- 10 ounces canned artichoke hearts, drained and chopped
- 6 ounces cream cheese
- 1/2 cup Greek-style yogurt
- 1/2 cup mayo
- 1/2 cup water
- 2 cloves garlic, minced
- 20 ounces Monterey-Jack cheese, shredded

Directions

1. Start by preheating your oven to 350 degrees F.
2. Combine all of the ingredients, except for the Monterey-Jack cheese. Place the mixture in a lightly greased baking dish.
3. Top with the shredded Monterey-Jack cheese. Bake in the preheated oven for 17 to 22 minutes or until bubbly. Serve warm.

65. Italian Cheese Crisps

Simple and fun, with just 5 minutes prep, these crisps are much better and healthier than classic potato chips or any other processed snack you can find.

Servings 4

Ready in about 10 minutes

NUTRITIONAL INFORMATION (Per Serving)

134 - Calories
11.1g - Fat
0.4g - Carbs
0g - Fiber
4.9g - Protein
0g - Sugars

Ingredients

- 1 cup sharp Cheddar cheese, grated
- 1/4 teaspoon ground black pepper
- 1/2 teaspoon cayenne pepper
- 1 teaspoon Italian seasoning

Directions

1. Start by preheating an oven to 400 degrees F. Line a baking sheet with a parchment paper.
2. Mix all of the above ingredients until well combined.
3. Then, place tablespoon-sized heaps of the mixture onto the prepared baking sheet.
4. Bake at the preheated oven for 8 minutes, until the edges start to brown. Allow the cheese crisps to cool slightly; then, place them on paper towels to drain the excess fat. Enjoy!

66. Deviled Eggs with Mustard and Chives

These stuffed eggs are perfect for party dinners and potlucks. A cook's note: Once the eggs are chilled, crack them and place in cold water for 10 minutes; the peels will come off much easier.

Servings 8

Ready in about
20 minutes +
chilling time

NUTRITIONAL
INFORMATION
(Per Serving)

149 - Calories
11.3g - Fat
1.6g - Carbs
0.1g - Fiber
9.4g - Protein
1g - Sugars

Ingredients

- 8 eggs
- 2 tablespoons cream cheese
- 1 teaspoon Dijon mustard
- 1 tablespoon mayonnaise
- 1 tablespoon tomato puree, no sugar added
- 1 teaspoon balsamic vinegar
- Sea salt and freshly ground black pepper, to taste
- 1/4 teaspoon cayenne pepper
- 2 tablespoons chives, chopped

Directions

1. Place the eggs in a single layer in a saucepan. Add water to cover the eggs and bring to a boil.
2. Cover, turn off the heat, and let the eggs stand for 15 minutes. Drain the eggs and peel them under cold running water.
3. Slice the eggs in half lengthwise; remove the yolks and thoroughly combine them with cream cheese, mustard, mayo, tomato puree, vinegar, salt, black, and cayenne pepper.
4. Next, divide the yolk mixture among egg whites. Garnish with fresh chives and enjoy!

67. Mini Stuffed Peppers

Who says stuffed peppers must be reserved for lunchtime? These mini spicy bites will delight your guests!

Servings 5

Ready in about 15 minutes

NUTRITIONAL INFORMATION (Per Serving)

198 - Calories
17.2g - Fat
3g - Carbs
0.9g - Fiber
7.8g - Protein
1.8g - Sugars

Ingredients

- 2 teaspoons olive oil
- 1 teaspoon mustard seeds
- 5 ounces ground turkey
- Salt and ground black pepper, to taste
- 10 mini bell peppers, cut in half lengthwise, stems and seeds removed
- 2 ounces garlic and herb seasoned chevre goat cheese, crumbled

Direction

1. Heat the oil in a skillet over medium-high heat. Once hot, cook mustard seeds with ground turkey until the turkey is no longer pink. Crumble with a fork. Season with salt and black pepper.
2. Lay the pepper halves cut-side-up on a parchment-lined baking sheet. Spoon the meat mixture into the center of each pepper half.
3. Top each pepper with cheese. Bake in the preheated oven at 400 degrees F for 10 minutes. Bon appétit!

DESSERTS

68. Almond Butter and Chocolate Cookies

This is no bake, keto-friendly, and simple dessert for any occasion! Use coconut oil cooking spray to lightly grease a baking sheet; it will allow you to easily cut and remove the squares from the baking sheet.

Servings 8

Ready in about 15 minutes + chilling time

NUTRITIONAL INFORMATION (Per Serving)

322 - Calories
28.9g - Fat
3.4g - Carbs
0.6g - Fiber
13.9g - Protein
0.7g - Sugars

Ingredients

- 1 stick butter
- 1/2 cup almond butter
- 1/2 cup Monk fruit powder
- 3 cups pork rinds, crushed
- 1 teaspoon vanilla extract
- 1/4 teaspoon ground cinnamon
- 1/2 cup sugar-free chocolate, cut into chunks
- 1/2 cup double cream

Directions

1. In a pan, melt the butter, almond butter, and Monk fruit powder over medium heat.
2. Now, add the crushed pork rinds and vanilla. Place the batter on a cookie sheet and let it cool in your refrigerator.
3. Meanwhile, in a small saucepan over medium heat, melt the chocolate and double cream. Add the chocolate layer over the batter.
4. Allow it to chill completely before slicing and serving. Bon appétit!

69. Basic Orange Cheesecake

This cheesecake tastes like everything you love about holiday season but without too many calories and sugar. In addition, this dessert doesn't require you to spend hours in the kitchen.

Servings 12

Ready in about 15 minutes + chilling time

NUTRITIONAL INFORMATION (Per Serving)

150 - Calories
15.4g - Fat
2.1g - Carbs
0.1g - Fiber
1.2g - Protein
1.9g - Sugars

Ingredients

Crust:
- 1 tablespoon Swerve
- 1 cup almond flour
- 1 stick butter, room temperature
- 1/2 cup unsweetened coconut, shredded

Filling:
- 1 teaspoon powdered gelatin
- 2 tablespoons Swerve
- 17 ounces mascarpone cream
- 2 tablespoon orange juice

Directions

1. Thoroughly combine all the ingredients for the crust; press the crust mixture into a lightly greased baking dish.
2. Let it stand in your refrigerator.
3. Then, mix 1 cup of boiling water and gelatin until all dissolved. Pour in 1 cup of cold water.
4. Add Swerve, mascarpone cheese, and orange juice; blend until smooth and uniform. Pour the filling onto the prepared crust. Enjoy!

70. Peanut Butter and Chocolate Treat

You can make this dessert in advance and store it in the freezer until ready to eat. Enjoy all the flavor without guilt!

Servings 10

Ready in about 10 minutes + chilling time

NUTRITIONAL INFORMATION (Per Serving)

122 - Calories
11.7g - Fat
4.9g - Carbs
1.4g - Fiber
1.5g - Protein
1.9g - Sugars

Ingredients

- 1 stick butter, room temperature
- 1/3 cup peanut butter
- 1/3 cup unsweetened cocoa powder
- 1/3 cup Swerve
- 1/2 teaspoon ground cinnamon
- A pinch of grated nutmeg
- 1/4 cup unsweetened coconut flakes
- 1/4 cup pork rinds, crushed

Directions

1. Melt the butter and peanut butter until smooth and uniform.
2. Add the remaining ingredients and mix until everything is well combined.
3. Line a baking sheet with a silicone baking mat. Pour the mixture into the baking sheet. Place in your freezer for 1 hour until ready to serve. Enjoy!

71. Coconut Cranberry Bars

One of nature's most fabulous gifts to us is a fresh and sweet fruit. Now, we're going to use coconut and cranberries and make these fabulous bars; with their soft and smooth texture, you will add a little touch of summer to your days.

Servings 12

Ready in about 1 hour 20 minutes

NUTRITIONAL INFORMATION (Per Serving)

107 - Calories
11.1g - Fat
2.5g - Carbs
0.9g - Fiber
0.4g - Protein
1.4g - Sugars

Ingredients

- 1/3 cup cranberries
- 1 ½ cups coconut flakes, unsweetened
- 1/2 cup butter, melted
- 1/2 teaspoon liquid Stevia

Directions

1. Mix all ingredients in your food processor until well combined. Press the batter into a baking sheet.
2. Refrigerate for 1 hour. Cut into bars and serve well chilled.

72. Peanut and Butter Cubes

With its soft and crunchy texture, these peanut cubes are a dessert lover's dream. You just can't get enough of them.

Servings 10

Ready in about 50 minutes

NUTRITIONAL INFORMATION (Per Serving)

218 - Calories
21.2g - Fat
5.1g - Carbs
0.7g - Fiber
3.8g - Protein
1.3g - Sugars

Ingredients

- 1 stick butter
- 1/3 cup coconut oil
- 1 vanilla paste
- 1/4 teaspoon cinnamon powder
- 2 tablespoons Monk fruit powder
- A pinch of coarse salt
- 1/2 cup peanuts, toasted and coarsely chopped

Directions

1. Microwave the butter, coconut oil, and vanilla until melted. Add cinnamon powder, Monk fruit powder, and salt.
2. Put the chopped peanuts into a silicon mold or an ice cube tray. Pour the warm butter mixture over the peanuts.
3. Place in your freezer for 40 to 50 minutes. Bon appétit!

73. Easiest Brownies Ever

If you do not want to use a microwave, just bring water to a simmer. Place the heatproof bowl over the pot with hot water; make sure the water doesn't touch the bowl. Place the chocolate in the bowl and stir periodically until it is melted.

Servings 10

Ready in about 1 hour

NUTRITIONAL INFORMATION (Per Serving)

205 - Calories
19.5g - Fat
5.4g - Carbs
3.2g - Fiber
4.7g - Protein
0.4g - Sugars

Ingredients

- 2 tablespoons almond flour
- 3 tablespoons coconut flour
- 1/2 teaspoon baking powder
- 1/2 cup cocoa powder, unsweetened
- 4 eggs
- 1/2 cup Swerve
- 1 teaspoon almond extract
- 1 vanilla extract
- 1/2 cup coconut oil
- 3 ounces baking chocolate, unsweetened

Directions

1. Thoroughly combine the almond flour, coconut flour, cocoa powder, and baking powder.
2. Mix in the eggs, Swerve, almond and vanilla extract; beat with an electric mixer on high until everything is well combined.
3. In a separate bowl, melt the coconut oil and chocolate in your microwave. Now, add the egg mixture and mix again.
4. Gradually add the dry ingredients and whisk until everything is well incorporated. Pour the batter into a lightly greased baking pan.
5. Bake in the preheated oven at 320 degrees F approximately 50 minutes or until a toothpick inserted into the middle of your brownie comes out clean and dry. Bon appétit!

74. No Bake Party Cake

The perfect party cake, Irish cream cheesecake is a classic dessert that everyone will love. It makes an easy birthday cake, too.

Servings 6

Ready in about 30 minutes

NUTRITIONAL INFORMATION (Per Serving)

274 - Calories
27.5g - Fat
5.7g - Carbs
1.6g - Fiber
3.8g - Protein
2.1g - Sugars

Ingredients

- 1/4 cup almond flour
- 1/4 cup coconut flour
- 2 tablespoons cocoa powder
- 1 ½ tablespoons Swerve
- 1 tablespoon almond butter
- 2 tablespoons coconut oil
- A pinch of salt
- A pinch of cinnamon powder
- 7 ounces mascarpone cheese
- 2 tablespoons coconut oil
- 2 tablespoons cocoa powder
- 1/4 cup tablespoons Swerve
- 1/3 cup double cream
- 2 tablespoons Irish whiskey
- 1 teaspoon vanilla extract
- 1/2 cup double cream
- 1 teaspoon grass-fed gelatin

Directions

1. In a small bowl, thoroughly combine the almond flour, coconut flour, cocoa, and Swerve.
2. Add almond butter, coconut oil, salt, and cinnamon powder; press the crust into a baking pan.
3. To make the filling, melt mascarpone cheese and coconut oil in a microwave for 40 seconds.
4. Add cocoa, Swerve, 1/3 cup of cream, Irish whiskey, and vanilla; beat with an electric mixer until creamy and uniform.
5. Then, whip 1/2 cup of double cream until it has doubled in volume.
6. In a small mixing bowl, combine gelatin with 1 tablespoon of cold water; whisk until dissolved. Now, add 1 tablespoon of hot water and stir until well combined.
7. Slowly and gradually, add dissolved gelatin to the whipped cream; mix until stiff. Now, fold the prepared whipped cream into the cream cheese mixture.
8. Spread the filling over the crust and serve well chilled. Enjoy!

75. Vanilla Mug Cake

All the ingredients are mixed together, and then your cakes cook in the microwave for about 1 minute. In addition, there are endless varieties of flavors; you can add fruits, cocoa, chocolate, and different spices. Easy!

Servings 2

Ready in about 10 minutes

NUTRITIONAL INFORMATION (Per Serving)

143 - Calories
10.7g - Fat
5.7g - Carbs
2.6g - Fiber
5.7g - Protein
2.8g - Sugars

Ingredients

- 4 tablespoons psyllium husk flour
- 2 tablespoons ground flax seed
- 5 tablespoons almond flour
- 4 tablespoons Monk fruit powder
- A pinch of salt
- A pinch of grated nutmeg
- 1 teaspoon baking soda
- 4 tablespoons full-fat milk
- 1 teaspoon vanilla paste

Directions

1. Thoroughly combine all of the above ingredients in lightly greased mugs.
2. Then, microwave your cakes for 1 minute. Bon appétit!

Made in the USA
San Bernardino, CA
30 March 2019